Ned

Pearls of Writing Wisdom

From 16 Shucking Years as a Columnist

Port Hole Publishing
Florence, Oregon and Polson, Montana

Pearls of Writing Wisdom, from 16 Shucking Years as a Columnist
by Ned Hickson

Copyright © 2016 by Ned Hickson
All rights reserved

First Paperback Edition © 2016
ISBN-10: 1-943119-06-6
ISBN-13: 978-1-943119-06-6

Published by   Port Hole Publishing
                179 Laurel St. - Suite D
                Florence, OR 97439
                541-999-5725

All rights reserved. No part of this book may be reproduced or transmitted in any form without written permission from the author, except in the manner of brief quotations embodied in critical articles and reviews. Please respect the author and the law and do not participate in or encourage piracy of copyrighted materials.

Every effort has been made to be accurate. The author assumes no responsibility or liability for errors made in this book.

Front cover photo by Joshua Greene.
Cover design by Eric Wilder of Wilder Designs.
Interior design by Suzanne Fyhrie Parrott.

Printed and bound
in the United States of America.

Acknowledgments

*For Mrs. Phillers, my college prep English teacher
who tearfully flunked me my freshman year of high school
and challenged me to take my writing seriously;
for Mr. Danielson, my sophomore English teacher
who taught me the importance of having a point to my writing;
for Bob Serra, the newspaper editor who took a chance
on hiring me as a journalist with no experience or college education;
for Ellen Traylor, my publisher, whose encouragement
is the reason for this book;*

*And for my wife, Alicia,
whose love and support inspires my every word.*

Where to Look for Pearls

Let's talk about writing. 5

When you can't *not* be a writer 8

In the beginning 15

Keeping perspective 25

Find and use your tools. 29

Establishing a dialogue 33

Define your style. 42

Take a step back. 53

Do you feel a draft? 59

A word on endings. 64

Are we there yet? 69

Technically speaking 77

Finding the good in rejection 82

Avoid too much, too fast. 89

Keeping your balance. 93

Finally, remember your superpowers 96

About the Author. 98

Let's talk about writing

There are nearly eight-billion people inhabiting the earth. Most (with the exception of lawyers) are capable of stringing together a sequence of words in order to communicate an idea that others can understand. But for the rest of us, if you were to log on to any social network at this very moment, you'd find thousands of people writing about a number of topics, including dating, sex, parenting, mental illness... (See a pattern?)

With all of these people writing, what determines the difference between someone who writes and a *writer*? As with any art form, deciding between "good" and "poor" writing comes down to personal taste and interpretation. But in the end, there is one thing that truly defines any artist:

His or her *voice*.

Let me preface what I'm about to say by admitting I know nothing about art. Yet I have great respect for any artist whose work can provoke me into seeing or understanding something in a different way. I once saw an art piece called "Eternal Hunger" which, cleverly, was an empty room with a single pea glued to the center of the floor. I remember standing there in the doorway and quietly reflecting to myself:

I'll probably never like peas.

As absurd as that exhibit may sound, I remember it because the artist's presentation — his voice — was confident and unique.

Did it change how I feel about peas?

No.

Am I still trying to swallow a pea my mom made me eat in 1972?

At this very moment.

My point is that writers are just like painters or sculptors; they have at their disposal tools to help them create and communicate in ways which — depending on how they use their tools and in what sequence — will resonate with their own unique voice. Establishing that voice not only takes understanding the tools you have and becoming proficient with them, but also being able to wield them with confidence. As writers, we are constantly faced with potential rejection. If you put your words out into the world for others to read, whether by an editor, spouse or blog reader, the risk of rejection is always there. That's not exactly an atmosphere conducive to building confidence, especially when you're first starting out.

Or if your spouse is a copy editor.

If you are a writer, or fear you might be one, I wrote this book for you. Within the following pages are pearls of writing wisdom: insights, tips and encouragement shucked from my 16 years as a newspaper columnist and writer. Many are things I wish someone had told me sooner; some are the result of trial and error; and a few are simple truths that helped me keep perspective through all these shucking years as a writer.

Think of this book as the conversation we'd have about writing if we were sharing a cold beer. We'd talk about technique, style, personal experiences and hopes. We'd encourage each other and share a few laughs. We might even get a little rowdy and start using air quotation marks. In the end, we'd feel inspired about our love of writing.

Except, at the end of this conversation, neither of us needs to call a cab when it's over.

So pull up a stool, turn the page and let's talk about writing…

Writing isn't a pursuit;
It finds you…

1
When you can't *not* be a writer

Not long ago, I had the chance to work with some young writers, one of whom asked me a familiar question: "Did you always want to be a writer?"

I smiled, nodded my head and replied, "Oh, *heck* no."

After an awkward silence, I went on to explain that I had been writing stories since I could chew a pencil eraser. And while writing has always been a part of me, it wasn't until making the conscious decision to give it up for a while, that I truly understood the importance of writing in my life – and how, without it, I wasn't completely me. Without that experience, I would still be thinking of writing as a pursuit, rather than what it really is:

Something that finds *you*.

I quit writing back in 2006 for almost a year. It had nothing to do with the typical kinds of frustration every writer faces, such as not having a readership or being told it's time to "get serious" with your life, by family, friends and every publisher on the West Coast. It wasn't the result of drug addiction or alcohol abuse, (although I did find myself addicted to watching *Grey's Anatomy*, which made me WANT to drink).

Things were going well with my writing. My readership was growing and I had an agent working to get me signed with a large publishing house. The problem came when I turned 40 and found myself a divorced single father with two young children at home. To make ends meet, I left the editorial department at our newspaper and went into sales. I also put my column on hiatus to focus on this transition in my life and the lives of my children. Most newspapers and their readers were understanding, even supportive. But not all of them were, and 20 newspapers stopped carrying my column. In addition, my first book deal was put on the back burner, where it eventually evaporated.

On the surface, the divorce seemed like the perfect inspiration for a columnist — at least until I sat down to write about it. I didn't want to become "the guy who writes about being divorced," but my life completely revolved around that subject at that point. At the same time, writing about superheated pickles and glow-in-the-dark mice seemed... trivial?

Silly, I know — but I wasn't myself then.

Because of the importance of that last statement, I'm going to repeat it: *I wasn't myself then*.

Even as I moved forward with my life, meeting and marrying the amazing woman I've been fortunate enough to call my wife for eight years now, something was still missing (and no, it has nothing to do with male pattern baldness):

It was *me*.

Not until the following summer did I find that piece of myself, when I returned to the newsroom and began writing my weekly column for the first time in nearly a year. A few weeks later, on my 41st birthday, I started a blog as part of a gradual return to what I love:

Writing about my editor behind her back.

Ha Ha! Just kidding!

I do that on Twitter.

Seriously, what I discovered between those two summers was how giving up my writing meant giving up that part of myself that makes me whole. For writers, the written word is how we process the world around us and, perhaps more importantly, how we define ourselves within it. While most people are content experiencing life with their five senses, writers have a sixth sense that has nothing to do with ghosts or M. Night ~~Shamalon Shamellon Shahma~~… *The Sixth Sense* guy. For writers, it's about those other five senses and sharing them with readers in a meaningful way — through serious reflection, humor, fiction or poetry.

In the same way that sharing life with my wife makes it real and complete, writing makes *me* real and complete. It's not that I couldn't survive without either one; I just don't ever want to.

As a writer, I'm sure you feel the same.

(But just so we're clear, my wife is off limits.)

It's been many years since I came out of the writing "closet." Or, in my case, the laundry room, which is where I did most of my writing until becoming a columnist in 1998. Before that, the same conversation replayed itself many times over the years, with family, friends and co-workers, most of whom thought of writing as something akin to collecting salt and pepper shakers; a "unique" hobby that I was asked not to talk about at parties.

"Don't take this the wrong way, but for people who don't know you — it makes them uncomfortable when your eyes light up like that when you talk about writing. It's kind of creepy."

The bottom line is that no one took my writing seriously. (Yes, I realize the irony of that statement, considering I am a humor columnist, but still…). In retrospect, there were many reasons why my wanting to be a writer was perceived as a bucket list item, rather than a legitimate goal. But truth be told, the problem lay in my own "wanting to be" a writer, instead of accepting that I *was* a writer.

We are conditioned from an early age to view money as a prime indicator of success and achievement. We use that measuring stick as validation, when it comes to pursuits that don't fall into traditional categories. In short: If you aren't getting paid for it, then you're not legitimate.

That's like saying you can't include "skydiving instructor" among the achievements in your obituary just because, on your last jump after 10 years as an instructor, your parachute didn't open. Even if you've landed flat on your face in terms of monetary or publishing success with your writing, it doesn't mean you aren't a writer; it just means there's a good possibility every publisher you submitted work to was a skydiving instructor who died before he could read your masterpiece.

I honestly can't tell you how many publishers plunged to their deaths before I saw my first words in print.

Regardless, if you spend time formulating words for the sheer enjoyment, while, at the same time, agonizing over those very same words, congratulations!

You are a writer!

How do I know this? Because people who are not writers would not put themselves through this process. Give the average person on the street a choice between writing five paragraphs about how they spent their summer, or being tased on the bare butt, and most will drop their pants. The ones who don't?

They're the writers.

The only legitimacy you need as a writer comes from *yourself* — and it starts with believing what you do is important and has value that isn't measured in dollars, or even common sense in the eyes of others. Let's face it, toiling alone over the choice and arrangement of words on a page doesn't make much sense to anyone who isn't a writer. People may nod their heads and smile when you try to explain it, but in their minds they're wondering if your choice to live so close to high-voltage power lines was a mistake. Again, the only thing that matters is giving *yourself* permission to take your writing seriously.

And by "seriously," I don't just mean you have a goal of getting published or paid for the words you write. I mean you take it seriously enough that you make time for it, in the same way you do other commitments that are important to your daily life. As I mentioned earlier, when I turned 40 I was a single father with two young children. As anyone with children knows, there's always something important that needs to be done. One night, while sitting in my study/laundry room, I realized two things, in exactly this order:

1) Until I started taking my writing seriously, no one else would,

and

2) By putting my daughter's favorite sweater through the dryer, it was now the perfect size for our neighbor's Chihuahua.

I couldn't do much about the sweater, which she's still bitter about 11 years later. But the first thing — taking my writing seriously — became a priority.

The first step was to establish a writing routine. In a way, establishing this routine is a lot like going to the gym. Except that you don't get sweaty, rarely leave a seated position and, unless you write romance or erotica, you probably won't increase your heart rate much. Aside from that, it's just like going to the gym.

When I first started writing in an actual newsroom, my routine consisted of sitting at my desk, staring blankly at the screen and banging on my keys as quickly as possible until it was time to go home, where I would do my actual writing.

Why did I do this?

I was intimidated. On either side of me, journalists were typing feverishly — seemingly non-stop — while I sat waiting for inspiration. My brain was hardwired for waiting until the kids were asleep before slinking off into the study/laundry room to do my writing. I'll admit, re-programming myself took time and persistence. I had to get over the fact that, as my fellow journalists were typing away, there were long periods of silence — some as long as 10 to 12 seconds — echoing from my cubicle. Eventually, my brain actually adapted to having a real writing schedule, much in the same way your body adapts to a workout routine. (I say "your body" because mine still hates going to the gym no matter what time it is.)

I realize not everyone has the luxury of writing full time. However, establishing a routine says something important:

I'm a writer and you're not, so neener neener!

Ok, not really.

...Well, actually, yes — but that's not my point.

Married or single, with or without kids, stay-at-home or away-at-work parent, full- or part-time job, setting a writing routine says to yourself and others that your writing is just as important as other responsibilities you have. Whether it's 30 minutes or three hours, every day or certain days of the week, making that commitment to yourself as writer — to write without exception, excuse or apology — is something you owe yourself as a writer. No one objects to your making dinner, mowing the lawn, doing laundry, ironing or picking up the kids after practice, and your writing routine shouldn't be any different.

Bottom line? If you take your writing seriously, so will others.

And if they don't? It doesn't make you any less a writer. Published or unpublished, novelist or columnist, fiction or non-fiction, accept yourself for being a writer and always make time for putting those words down on paper. It is both a gift and a responsibility, and it is a pursuit that is uniquely your own to determine and discover. Make it part of your lifestyle and treasure those who embrace it with you.

For everyone else? I hear that skydiving makes a great holiday gift.

Step one to becoming a writer:
Write.

2
In the beginning

The notion that being a writer means you actually have to *write* seems pretty straight forward. However, unless you're careful, it's the kind of obvious straight forwardness that can carry you with complete confidence toe-first into a brick. Like most advice we're given, the wisdom behind the notion is simple; the problem comes in the execution. While there are countless books out there offering tips on everything from how to get inspired and avoid "writer's block," to the kinds of foods that promote creative thinking (which, judging from what I read, will require you to do most of that thinking on the commode), all of those books essentially come down to one universal truth:

The fastest way to jump-start the writing process is to put your fingers to the keyboard and just start writing.

Occasionally, I make it a point to sit down and write my column without any preparation. I do this to 1) challenge myself, and 2) because sometimes I really have no idea what I am going to write until I have a deadline breathing down my neck. So I just start writing.

Do I take a wrong turn or two?

Absolutely.

But the beauty of writing is that — like with the Kardashians — nothing is permanent, and you can easily fix imperfections by injecting or removing the things you don't like. And many times, what you thought was going to be a wrong turn or dead end leads to a doorway you hadn't expected — or at least a window you can jump out of.

Let's see a show of hands from those who have ever found themselves staring at a blank screen with their fingers poised over the keyboard, even if they have applied my advice?

Seriously, I'm watching, so get those hands up.

There's nothing quite like staring at a blank page, knowing that with a few strokes of the keyboard you will transform a landscape devoid of life into a living, breathing thing of your own creation. There's also nothing quite like finishing that fourth cup of coffee only to find that same blank page staring back at you. Sure, you may have typed several sentences — or maybe even the same sentence several times — in hopes of gaining some kind of momentum to carry you over that first hump, but the cursor repeatedly stalls out in the same spot, leaving you with the same blank page after riding the "delete" button back to the beginning.

Hey, that's why it's called a "cursor."

I'll be honest: I don't necessarily subscribe to the notion of "writer's block," which suggests some kind of blockage — such as a cheese wedge or too many butter biscuits — restricting movement through a hypothetical colon of creativity. Although there are some books that offer evidence to support at least part of the colon theory, I prefer to think of the writing process as cells in a battery; when they are fully charged, things start easily. But if the alternator belt slips too much or the terminals get corroded, you end up without enough juice to turn the engine.

Because we are writers and not mechanics, and because that last sentence exhausted the full extent of my automotive knowledge, I will sum up my analogy with this: When your battery is low, you need a jump, right?

Writing is no different.

That being said, I have been asked by my lawyer to clarify that this does not mean anyone should actually hook jumper cables to any part of his or her anatomy and ask a friend to crank the engine. For those of you who have already tried this, you can back me up. The rest of you will just have to take my word for it.

Obviously, there are lots of reasons your creativity may need a jump start once in a while, whether it be from a lack of sleep or simple distractions, worries or even injury – possibly involving jumper cables.

Speaking of which, here is one more automotive reference we need to address:

Fuel.

It doesn't matter how many times you twist the ignition, the engine won't start without fuel. The same thing goes for getting your brain to fire on all cylinders. That doesn't mean you have to set up your laptop next to the carving station at a breakfast buffet. Although it will give you unfettered access to the ham.

The point is, make sure you eat before you settle in to write. Should it be a balanced meal? Who cares! We're grown-ups! We can eat a mixing bowl full of Fruity Pebbles between lunch and dinner if we want! Whatever you do, don't write on an empty stomach. Especially in the morning, even if you just have a cup of coffee and three chocolate chip cookies. (Which, by the way, is a purely random example, and has no correlation to what I ate before writing this. Particularly if my wife is reading.)

So, let's assume you are fueled up and you've settled in to write. And let's further assume you have almost finished that first cup of coffee and the cursor is still blinking at you on a blank page. And let's additionally assume the buffet has ended and you have been asked to leave because brunch is now over and it's time to set up for happy hour. Then try one or more of these suggestions to get your creative engine cranking:

1) Start your day with social media interaction.

Something I've discovered from writing a daily blog is that the interaction with other writers on blogs and websites – whether replying to a comment or leaving one on another writer's site — can be a great way to spark the creative process. Starting your day with some social interaction at your computer not only gets you into writing position at the keyboard, but reading others' work or formulating responses can inspire your creativity.

Warning: Set a time limit!

As I can attest, it's easy to lose track of time, or become so caught up in commenting and replying that your momentum is carried in the wrong direction. I usually give myself until I finish my first cup of coffee. Which, by the way, I have switched from the giant 128-ounce Big Gulp size to a standard mug. Not only because I was using it as an excuse to blog until noon, but also because I discovered my bladder only holds 120 ounces.

2) Read someone else's work you admire or blatantly dislike.

Whether you read the work of a blogger, columnist or novelist, someone who inspires you can serve as a reminder of what good writing can do. And while it's true that it can backfire by also reminding you of how much your writing stinks by comparison, or how being a humor columnist isn't taken as seriously as a boring political analyst who never says anything remotely funny because he's too busy cashing his enormous paycheck and talking with influential people… it's still a really fun way to get those creative juices flowing! In the same way, reading someone whose work you dislike can spark your creativity by inspiring you to write even better and having it acknowledged by your reading audience. Even if that audience is only the stuffed animals from your kid's room that you have assembled at the kitchen table for that purpose.

(Again, that's just a random example that has nothing to do with me.)

3) Google a random image and write a story for it.

Sometimes the best way to focus in on your writing is to change your focus for a short period. Think of this exercise as looking through the lens of a camera and purposely blurring the image so you can better appreciate reality when you see it. One way to do this with your writing is to pick a topic — romance, humor, drama, action — and Google images for it, i.e., "romantic images" or "action images." Once they come up, give yourself a limit — say three pages — to look through and pick one image. Then give yourself 15 minutes to create either dialogue or a brief story-line to go with it.

Not only will this get your mind working but, occasionally, it can spark an entirely new story idea. Especially if you find an unflattering image of yourself on the Internet you didn't know existed, such as one of you wearing nothing but a pot holder over your privates while passed out in the pool on an inflatable whale.

(Once again, this is a completely random example with no connection to me personally.)

4) Pick a song that inspires you and sing it at the top of your lungs.

Most of us have a musical device of some kind with our favorite tunes on it. Pick a song that always makes you feel good, go somewhere you can sing freely — such as the bedroom, a hiking trail, Starbucks — and put in your ear-buds. Then sing LOUDLY! Music inspires our creativity in a way nothing else does. Feel the music and, if necessary, sing it loudly more than once! Or even while running from the police! I actually listen to AC/DC whenever I write. My habit of singing "T.N.T." loudly before I write has not only helped spark my creativity, it has also sparked discussion in the newsroom about giving me my own office.

Possibly across the street.

There are a lot of writers who see writing inspiration as a mystical process sparked by their personal muses. When you consider that there were nine Muses in Greek mythology, you'd think finding yours would be pretty easy. The Muses, as you probably know, were all extraordinarily beautiful women (remember, philosophers were all men back then), with names like Fallopia, Urethra, Tetracycline, Chlamydia, Herpes, etc., and were the daughters of mighty Zeus and the goddess of personified memory… uh, whose name escapes me.

Each muse served as inspiration for different art forms, such as literature, oration, sculpture, music, Reuben sandwiches and others.

I realize I have now probably guaranteed that my muse is hovering over our unsuspecting copy editor who, at this moment, is jotting down an outline for the next blockbuster literary franchise. But that's OK! I like our copy editor. If she achieves fame and fortune with the help of my vengeful muse, I will be happy for her.

I won't buy her stupid book, but I'll be happy for her.

However, given that I'm Danish and not Greek, I've never subscribed to the idea of a muse, no matter how much Greek yogurt I shovel down my throat. As a columnist, I look to several sources of inspiration each day while, at the same time, trying to keep an eye out for inspiration in unlikely places. Often, it's the unlikely that provides the most interesting perspective. Here are a few of the places I begin my day:

News reports

Given that I work at a newspaper, my iPad has a CNN feed. Not just because we're too cheap to have an Associated Press membership, but also so I can keep up on important breaking news, such as the latest on North Korea's threat to launch nuclear missiles at Canada for giving us Justin Bieber…

OK, sure. We all know that's not an *actual* news story (yet), but by combining the first two headlines that came up on my CNN feed, it sparked an idea. Whether it could catch fire remains to be seen. The important thing is that Canada — and the world's maple syrup supply — are safe.

Morning conversations

I admit it: I'm an eavesdropper. When I go to the coffee shop in the morning, I listen for key phrases in other people's conversations. I'm not necessarily listening for information as much as the exchange of ideas and opinions. Many times, other people's perspectives, particularly if they are uninformed or one-sided, have given me ideas for columns, characters or dialogue. In addition, there have been times when my misunderstanding of what was being talked about led to an idea. For example, I once wrote a column on how a Chihuahua had been called to jury duty in Los Angeles because its owners had obtained a social security number for it in order to claim it as a dependent…

Uh, wait. Sorry – that really *did* happen. I just thought I misunderstood the conversation. But hey, it happened in Los Angeles! I should have known better!

Anyway, you'll notice I specifically said "morning" conversations. That's because people tend to be more relaxed in the morning, before they head to work, and well before the day's stress has set in. They are fresh or, quite possibly, a little hung over. What comes out of their mouths is generally more interesting than what comes out at the end of the day. Assuming they aren't competitive eaters.

Advertisements

Whether it's newspaper or magazine advertising, television or radio, how many times have you found yourself shaking your head thinking, "The side effects are worse than the symptoms!" or "Do that many people really suffer from unsightly ear hair?" or "Why is it that TV commercial husbands are always balding and overweight while their wives look like fitness instructors?" You might say these questions have nothing to do with finding your muse, but actually you can find inspiration in advertising.

I recently heard a radio ad offering treatment for TSAD (Teen-aged Social Anxiety Disorder). Symptoms include: a lack of confidence, irritability, mood swings and resistance to family outings. Thinking back on my teen-aged years, being told we were going on a family outing was like hearing I had just sat on a petri dish in a level-four bio-hazard lab; my hope was that death would be mercifully quick. My point? This commercial got me thinking – a condition for which the only available treatment is to write about it.

As a writer, recognizing and developing story ideas is your bread and butter. Or biscuits and gravy, depending on your proximity to the Mason-Dixon line. The point is, whether you are a romance novelist, sci-fi short story writer or weekly columnist, generating ideas – and recognizing the difference between good ones and not-so-good ones (there are no completely bad ideas in my opinion, and I'll explain why in a moment) – is the most important skill you must develop.

> **Warning:** *Keep in mind that while today's wireless, techno-savvy world of instant access information can be a bottomless well of inspiration for any writer – just like the school immunization records for Brad and Angelina's children – it can also swallow you whole in its vastness.*

Every writer has his or her own technique when it comes to inspiration, and the Internet is only one part of a much larger equation. While I certainly scan through headlines from the larger Portland and Eugene newspapers in an effort to stay up on cultural trends and world events, once I leave the office restroom I generally refer to a collection of ideas I keep in a folder on my desk. In it, I have clippings, printouts, emails and ideas jotted on pieces of paper.

So how do I decide between good ideas and not-so-good ones? Before we get to that, I will explain why, as I mentioned earlier, I don't believe there are any "bad" ideas.

At least when it comes to writing.

When I went skateboarding down "suicide hill" wearing nothing but swim trunks and flip-flops when I was 10? That was definitely a bad idea.

When it comes to cultivating story ideas – good or "bad" – they're all part of the filtration process. Think of "bad" ideas as corn mash: it isn't what you're after when making moonshine, but it's a by-product of the fermentation process that leads to the end result. The trick is knowing when to dump it, even though, like whiskey, mash can still get you intoxicated. (Or so I've heard.)

On my desk is a folder I have cleverly labeled: Column Ideas.

This folder contains my "corn mash." That's where everything goes to begin the fermentation process. Like a bootlegger, I sift through it regularly, dumping what is no longer usable (because of timeliness issues or spilled coffee, for example) and adding more in its place. On those occasions where I come into the office without an idea (like Mondays through Fridays), I turn to this folder to see if anything is ready to begin the distillation process. Sometimes just a key phrase in something I saved will spark an idea. And even though it may not be directly related to the idea in the folder, again, it started with the corn mash.

I should point out that there are definitely ideas that I act upon without ever going near my folder. For example, I received an email last week from…

God.

He apparently lives in San Mateo, Calif., and has a P.O. box.

These are the kinds of things I really have no choice but to write about immediately. And not just because I might land the lead in "Ned Almighty."

So whether you keep a notebook to jot down ideas, search the Internet, notice an interesting exchange in a restaurant while sipping coffee, or inadvertently catch site of something suspicious at your neighbors' house, once the binoculars are put away write these things down and let them begin the fermentation process.

These are some of the ways you can find inspiration. As a writer, you are already hardwired for observation. Whether you're in the coffee shop, your child's pre-school, the local post office or somewhere completely unexpected, your "muse" is always waiting.

Assuming it hasn't gone off in search of some Greek yogurt.

The key to survival as a writer: Wield your tools

3
Keeping perspective

Over the years, my wife has gotten used to my admittedly bad habit of leaning over and whispering *expendable character* whenever I see someone who I know is going to die. I should clarify I only make these predictions while watching movies, and not, as a general rule, at the grocery store, in hospital waiting rooms or at family reunions. That's because, in movies, these types of characters are easy to spot.

For example, the soldier who pulls out a photo of his "girl back home" while talking with his buddy on patrol —

Spoiler Alert: He's not making it through the next scene alive. And if he mentions he's proposing to "his girl" after getting discharged tomorrow? Chances are he won't even finish his dinner rations before keeling over from sniper fire or eating expired creamed corn.

The same goes for anyone who mentions having a "bad ticker" or who has a nagging cough; anyone who says he's stopped wearing a bullet-proof vest or life jacket because "you can't cheat fate"; and definitely any character who keeps a mouse or baby bird his shirt pocket.

The same can be said for recognizing the difference between writers who utilize survivor skills and those who are setting themselves up to be "expendable." Let's face it, at this very moment there are about as many writers clanking on keyboards as there are fictional characters out there.

Keeping a healthy perspective on your writing and its place in the world can be tough, unless you define who you are as a writer. To do that, you must find your own writing "voice" and learn to use the tools that will clarify and project it to others. If you do that, you'll be one of the writers eating creamed corn long after it has expired.

Before we get to the tools of establishing a writer's voice, I want you to keep the following things in mind as part of maintaining a perspective that will ensure your survival:

Don't write for publication:

First, let's talk about what I'm *not* saying here. I'm not saying you shouldn't have hopes of being a published author or working toward the goal of writing for a living, if that's your dream. If your heart pounds a little faster at the thought of seeing your book in print, never give up that dream. However, what I *am* saying is those thoughts should always be secondary to your writing itself. It's like the old saying about putting the cart before the horse. (Except in this case the horse is a pregnant three-legged Chihuahua with trust issues.) Unless you've hitched your cart to something real that you can count on and believe in, every day, you're not going to get very far. And there's nothing more real than your love for writing. Put that first, and your cart will keep moving forward.

(I'd lose the Chihuahua, though.)

Understand that size isn't important:

And no, this doesn't only apply to men.

The true measure of any writer's success has less to do with the size of his or her readership, and more to do with mastering a unique personal style. In the same way that dating a lot of people won't lead to a lasting relationship until you can define who you are as a person, connecting with readers interested in forging a long-term relationship won't happen until you can define who you are as a writer.

Survivors recognize the importance of this process, and readers recognize a writer who has taken the time to develop style and technique. It won't matter to them how large your readership is.

By the way, just to be clear...I'm 6-foot-1 with an average-sized readership, but thanks to style and technique I do OK.

We'll just leave it at that.

Remember who you're writing for:

This point really has two parts, both of which are equally important, and neither of which involves anyone related to publishing. There are really only two people you should be writing for every time you sit at the keyboard:

Yourself.

Your reader.

That first person you're writing for – You – seems pretty obvious. Over time, however, it can get forgotten as more people become involved in your writing process. Most of us started writing as kids or teens, back when the thrill of articulating our thoughts sparked a fire that burns today. It didn't matter if anyone else ever laid eyes on your work; you were writing for *you*, and that excitement came from a pure love and a desire to create.

To be a writing survivor, you have to remember that feeling and where it comes from. Those who don't aren't likely to survive the creamed corn.

The second person you need to be writing for is your reader. Again, it sounds pretty obvious – and it is. But sometimes I take it a step further and literally think of a specific reader as I write.

Oftentimes it's my wife. Other times I'll think of a reader who may have emailed me or stopped by my blog to offer a comment – positive or otherwise.

(My wife, however, is the only one I picture naked. Which I admit isn't particularly productive...

...

…
…)

Sorry, where was I?

Oh, yeah!

Anyone who has been involved in a theater knows how the energy level rises once you have a live audience. The same goes for writing. In this case, keeping a specific reader in mind can add a level of anticipation that sharpens your prose and helps you dig a little deeper.

On the surface, this may seem contrary to the first half of this section: Write for yourself. However, no matter who your readers are — wife, friends, complete strangers, cell mate — they are an extension of you as a result of the connection you've made through your writing.

Writers who take the time to define themselves write for themselves, and they recognize the relationship they have built with readers is not expendable.

With that in mind, let's roll up our sleeves and wield the tools and techniques that will help define and project your own unique writing voice.

I promise I won't sing.

4
Find and use your tools

My father was a collector of tools. His workshop had everything from compression wrenches to ohm meters and plumber's putty. Though he knew how to use all of them, there were certain tools he kept in his tool box because they were the ones he used most often. (Coincidentally, they were also the ones I was most likely to lose somewhere.)

As writers, we also have countless tools at our disposal. Over the last 16 years, I've assembled my own writer's tool box, containing those I use most, whether it's for repairing broken sentence structure or tightening some leaky prose — either of which can lead to faulty writing.

These first three I keep in the top tray of my tool box, right next to the duct tape:

Timing:

To me, this is among the most important and frequently wielded tools of a writer. It's also the most complex, because so many factors play a role in timing, including punctuation, paragraph structure, word usage and even font choice.

As a humor columnist, I often want to take my readers by surprise, so that they don't see the punch line coming; much like a bullfighter who uses his cape to entrance a bull while, simultaneously, hiding the stain in the seat of his leotards.

Punctuation can offer the pause, beat or — as with the long dash — a visual distraction to hide the fact that, once again, I've forgotten my point.

Oh right… Timing. It can also be used to underscore a dramatic moment, or build tension and anticipation toward a climactic revelation your reader can't get to fast enough. To be a good storyteller around the campfire you have to relay information through use of inflection, pauses and occasional sound effects to add emphasis. It's the same with writing: how you utilize punctuation and sentence structure are as important as the words you choose in telling your story.

The best way to learn timing is by experimenting with it. Unlike the next two tools, *Truth* and *Relativity*, timing is mostly subjective. Like choosing the right color from an artist's palette; your choice may be different from mine, but we both know when it's right for us.

Truth:

More than any time in history, readers are astute at recognizing a false tone in writing. Reality TV shows, blogs and instant access to information have, to a certain degree, trained readers to be skeptics, making your job of building a connection with the reader particularly crucial. This is as true for columnists as it is for short-fiction writers (or even tall ones), who must build that connection within the first few paragraphs. This is especially important when it comes to fiction novels, where you are often asking readers to suspend their disbelief and buy into something — such as an eccentric character, over-the-top situation — that requires a leap of faith. In this case, your readers are making a "leap" over reality because they have faith that you, the writer, will keep them safely suspended until they land safely on the last page. That's assuming your book doesn't end with, "…Then there was a massive explosion and everybody died, including the basket of puppies."

As with taking any kind of leap, you must first gain momentum through a series of confident and quickening footfalls along a solid foundation. This applies to your writing as much as it does, hypothetically, to clearing the front fence of your home in order to beat your son to the restroom after a long car ride. Without the right amount of momentum, your reader could end up — again, hypothetically speaking — doing the splits on a picket fence.

The most effective way for a writer to build a reader's momentum toward a leap of faith is through writing that resonates with an underlying truth and honesty. This doesn't mean confessing how you re-named areas of Mrs. Flunkem's 7th-grade world map with parts of the reproductive system (although changing "Panama Canal" to "Fallopian Tube" is worth mentioning). No, when it comes to honesty in fiction writing I'm referring to what I like to call the "Double-D" approach (and not for reasons you might think). In this case we're referring to "dialogue" and "description" that ring true enough to establish believability and lay the foundation of confidence your reader will need when asked to make that leap with you. This applies equally to completely fictional characters, real people written within a fictional context, and even the persona writers project on blogs and social media sites.

We'll come back to *Dialogue* and *Description* in a bit.

Being truthful also means doing your homework by educating yourself before you write about something. For example, when I wrote about the first marriage proposal in space, I prepared myself by going through NASA's extensive astronaut training program.

OK, not really…

But I *did* do my research and discovered that I would not attend any wedding in space because the food would be those really terrible little packet thingys. Plus, throwing rice or birdseed, while a popular tradition, would mean spending the entire day surrounded by clouds of rice and seeds floating in zero gravity.

Write about what you know. Educate yourself about your subject so that readers will trust you.

The third tool is really an extension of Trust.

Relativity:

Even if you are already knowledgeable or experienced on a subject, you will lose your readers if they can't relate. This includes writing about personal experience; if the reader doesn't feel included, it won't matter how wacky "Aunt Frita's" romp through the bowling alley was if your reader doesn't know "Aunt Frita" is actually a mule.

I realize that's a bit of an overstatement, especially since I don't know "Aunt Frita" either, but without carefully laying the foundation in a way that includes your readers, they will likely sit down and refuse to follow. Think of your writing as a conversation; you must convey enough information for the other person to become invested in it. Many times, that means educating a reader about a subject, circumstance or individual through narrative.

When writing narrative dialogue, don't allow yourself to fall into "lecture" mode. We don't like it from our parents, teachers, bosses, ex-wives, etc., and readers don't either. Always keep your reader in mind. Pause every few paragraphs or minutes, depending on how fast you type (total elapsed time for this paragraph: three days) and ask yourself:

If I were having this conversation on the street with a stranger, what would he be thinking right now? Would she have questions? What feedback would he give? If someone drove by on a motor scooter, would she yank him off and steal the scooter just to get away?

You are building a relationship with your reader and, as with any good relationship, the other person needs to feel acknowledged. You can do this different ways, including throwing a question directly into your narrative.

See what I mean?

It's a way to break out of the lecture mode and invite the reader into the conversation.

I know what you're thinking: "Is he always this verbose, or is it just the coffee?"

Narrative "dialogue" should be just that: narrative established as dialogue with your readers that makes them feel included or acknowledged in the conversation.

5
Establishing a dialogue

Dialogue is one of the fastest ways to earn — or lose — a reader's trust. Whether it's your voice as a columnist or words spoken by someone in a novel or short story, you are essentially having a conversation with your readers asking them to "believe." And just like that guy at your office who is always talking about his crazy dating schedule with dozens of women when, in fact, you took your kids to the dollar theater Friday night and saw him sitting alone watching "Frozen 2," you know he's full of Whoppers. The same goes for your readers if the dialogue isn't believable.

Dialogue is used to convey many things, from mood to information, plot points to character profiles. Because writing dialogue is complex, for now I'm focusing specifically on ways to make your dialogue — whether character driven or as author narrative — ring true with your reader. Later on, we'll talk *Active Description* and the difference between "telling and showing," avoiding too many "he said, she said" references and the common mistake of nonsensical action dialogue.

For example:

"I'm LEAVING!" he yelled, slamming the door on her still-parted lips poised in reply.

Ouch. *rubs lips*

You have to think of your dialogue as a caricature, making sure to include specific details of the character's speech pattern — choice of words, cadence, vocabulary — that readers will come to recognizable as theirs. Just as a caricature artist relies on key physical traits that distinguish one individual from another, you must do the same when sketching out dialogue. When we meet new people, we instinctively study them to determine how far the relationship will extend. Acquaintance? Confidante? If there are inconsistencies in their behavior, such as explaining how they own a Porsche dealership yet leave Taco Bell driving a 1987 Ford Fiesta, we tend to question their honesty. The same goes for character dialogue. Readers study it and quickly form an opinion. If the character's vocabulary isn't consistent, or he speaks in bullet points one minute, then in long Shakespearean soliloquies the next, you'll lose your reader's trust. So take time to determine the nuances of your character's speech pattern in the same way you would his physical appearance and back-story.

Or backside.

Or whatever.

The second part of writing believable dialogue has nothing to do with what the character is saying, and everything to do with what he is doing while saying it. Which brings us to a… **POP QUIZ!**

The term "active description" refers to:

A. When a writer, who is seeking to lose weight and get published, writes a novel while riding a stationary bike;

B. Long paragraphs describing the sweat-filled pores of someone doing something exhausting.

C. Using a character's subtle actions and habits to help define him or her, and break up monotonous dialogue tags, such as "He said," used over and over again in a repeatedly repetitious fashion many, many times.

(Please explain your answer on the back of this book)

If you picked "C," give yourself a gold star and bring this book with you to the front of the class. If you picked either "A" or "B," give yourself a gold star anyway because no one fails here. Unless it's me doing a face-plant while pole dancing.

Active description is a way to add another level of believability to a character through the subtle nuances of how he moves her body language and actions. It's also an effective tool in breaking up dialogue patterns that quickly begin to feel contrived or repetitious. Lastly, it relays information about the character in ways that feel natural to us in actual conversation. Remember: What is being said is only half the conversation. The other half is the non-verbal communication happening at the same time. The more you can capture that feeling in your writing, the more believable your characters will be.

Here's an example of using dialogue and active description together to create a believable character. In this case, I was asked to write a mock "interview" with actor Kevin Spacey for a comedy blog that was hosting the real Kevin Spacey on its podcast. To prepare for it, I did some research on Spacey and learned he's a big fan of Mexican food, which is why I held the "interview" in a Mexican restaurant. I also discovered he produced a movie called "Albino Alligator," which flopped, but he apparently has a sense of humor about. At least I hope he does. I also watched several TV interviews in order to study his real-life way of talking and how he carries himself.

Here's a snippet:

…Spacey graciously offered me a seat before settling into his, legs crossed, one arm resting on the chair-back, leaving the other free to rummage through a basket of taco chips. This was clearly my signal to start the interview, which I did with a question that had been nagging me:

"Why did you agree to this interview and our podcast? It seems like one would be bad enough."

Spacey smiled and examined a chip, then quickly popped it into his mouth. "Did you ever see the movie Albino Alligator?" he asked, referring to his directorial debut, which grossed $339,000 and cost $6 million to make.

"Um… of course. It was great!"

"Bingo," said Spacey. "I owed you one."

Before I could ask my next question, a waiter approached the table for our order. Spacey, noted for his Hollywood impressions, chose to forgo the nacho bar and order from the menu as Clint Eastwood.

"I know what you're thinking," said Spacey, who squinted and began speaking through clenched teeth. "Will he order the number six chimichanga platter or only five. In all this confusion I sort of lost track myself. So I gotta ask myself: Do I feel lucky?"

"Well – DO you, PUNK?!?" I chimed in, then immediately regretted it.

The waiter gave me a nervous glance.

"A man's got to know his limitations, Ned" said Spacey.

To establish believability in this mock interview with Spacey, I opened up with active description that establishes his natural intensity and self-assuredness in order to add credibility to his dialogue – which is quick and direct. Just like the way he would eat his chip; no tiny bites, but in one quick pop. Also, by describing the way he took to his chair, crossed his legs and threw one arm over the chair back, all in quick succession, I established a decisive man who knows he wants to leave one hand free for grabbing chips long before he even sits down.

In contrast, here's a snippet from another mock "interview," this time with Clay Aiken. Once again, I did my research and set our "meeting" in his home town of Raleigh, N.C., then let his actions lend credibility to his dialogue – and build trust with readers to take this fun leap of faith with me…

>   *…As I sat on the back of his Bedazzled Vespa motor scooter, Aiken seemed to take pride in his city, as well as take corners so sharply I had to squeeze his waist. Though he had formally announced his bid for Congress a week before, Aiken told me more than once that he's no politician.*
>
>   *"I'm no politician!" he shouted over his shoulder, then swerved to avoid a cloud of mosquitoes. "Woooo! Shields down!"*
>
>   *Some speculate that his run against Republican incumbent Renee Ellmers is a publicity stunt aimed at putting him back in the spotlight for the release of his next album, Aiken for Change, which happens to be his campaign slogan. When asked about this, the American Idol star abruptly brought the scooter to a stop in a rundown South Raleigh neighborhood known for its high crime rate and low employment. He removed his helmet and raised an index finger, prepared to reply with a well-thought rebuttal, then quickly put his helmet back on.*
>
>   *"Oh darn," he whispered. "I didn't mean to stop in THIS neighborhood!"*

In case you're wondering, none of my research suggested Clay Aiken actually owns a Bedazzled Vespa motor scooter; that was part of my own leap of faith.

There are a couple of other key components to creating believable characters through dialogue and active description, as well as engaging narrative, that sometimes take a back seat. I'm talking about *Vocabulary* and *Economy*, which should be crammed into the front seat with everyone else — even if it means sharing the seat belt.

Vocabulary seems straight forward, right? Words used to communicate. Knowing a lot of words — or even big words — is less important than knowing the *right* words. Think of it as the care you put into choosing the words to express your love for someone. Or quite possibly to get out of a speeding ticket. In either case, there's a lot riding on your word selection. One wrong word, or too many of them, and you could find yourself in hand cuffs. (I realize for some of you that might be the actual objective, but just play along.)

In the last chapter, while talking about how research adds a level of truth and honesty in narrative and dialogue, I mentioned writing about the first marriage proposal in space:

> "…when I wrote about the first marriage proposal in space, I prepared myself by going through NASA's extensive astronaut training program."

What if I had written it like this?

> "…when I wrote my column on the first person to propose in space a while ago, I learned about the subject by participating in the astronaut program at NASA."

This is where vocabulary (choosing the right words) and economy (knowing what to omit) play an important role in your narrative writing.

Stop! Hammer time!

Let's break it down… and dissect that sentence by comparing the two:

> "…when I wrote my column"

versus

> "…when I wrote about…"

In the second instance, I'm assuming you already know it's "my column." I wanted to avoid another "me" reference and also improve the flow, so I eliminated "my column" from the sentence.

> "… on the first person to propose in space a while ago…"

versus

> "…the first wedding proposal in space…"

We all know it's a person who is proposing since there has been no reference to aliens or talking animals, so I didn't feel it was necessary to refer to "the first person" proposing. Instead, I went with "first wedding proposal in space" since the proposal is the subject. Now, if alien or talking-dog proposals were common place, then I would make sure to clarify it was a person proposing. Hopefully to another person and not a talking dog. And I chose to completely drop "a while ago" because it really doesn't matter when I wrote it, and cutting it cleaned up the sentence without losing any important information.

"…I learned about the subject by participating in the astronaut program at NASA"

versus

"…I prepared myself by going through NASA's extensive astronaut training program."

To get to the action of this sentence, I dropped "learned about" and "by participating in" and combined it into "preparing myself by going through." Then, I moved "NASA" closer to the action as a way to bring those two images together much faster. From that point, I built on the satire by describing what I did as "extensive astronaut training."

Are you having flashbacks from eighth-grade sentence diagramming? Sorry about that. But I hope this breakdown was helpful in offering at least some insight into the thought process of choosing the right words or, if nothing else, why my daughter won't let me anywhere near her book reports. Choosing the right word can often mean fewer words. Economy is big part of the revision process as you take a hard look at what can be eliminated from the literary structure while maintaining its integrity. Though this may not seem quite as important in longer works, it is critical for columnists, short-story writers and journalists. Every story requires being as concise as possible, using an economy of words.

And no, the irony that this is the biggest chapter in this book hasn't escaped me.

Fortunately, *Hypocrisy* isn't one of the tools we'll be covering.

Alfred Hitchcock once said everything in a movie must have purpose and propel the story. If it doesn't, it needs to be eliminated — which could explain the number of murders in his films. In short, when it comes to Economy, think of Alfred Hitchcock.

But probably not while you're in the shower.

Find your voice.

Then define it.

6
Define your style

During the previous two chapters, we zoned in on the specifics of creating a connection with readers through *Timing*, *Truth*, *Relativity*, *Dialogue*, *Active Description*, *Vocabulary* and *Economy*. We've dissected sentences and looked at how each of these tools plays a role in defining your voice as a writer. We've even discussed how writing while in the Lotus position with a bottle of Jack Daniels is the path to cosmic creativity.

Sorry, just checking to see who skipped a chapter.

Now let's talk about the importance of choosing the right *Narrative Voice* for your writing.

Here's a quick overview of the four main voices authors use when writing:

1) **Omniscient** — This is the all-seeing God-like voice, which was coincidentally used by my ex-wife. Haha! Just kidding! (She probably heard

that). This voice allows the author unlimited access to any character, timeframe, observation and inner monologue…

I am the all-powerful, all-knowing Omniscient Voice! I can be anywhere I want, any time I want, with access to anything I want, including any gas station restroom without lugging a key attached to the rim of a 1974 Gremlin!

2) **First Person** — For many reasons, this is the most common voice writers use. It establishes a sense of immediacy and connection by allowing the author to speak from a singular perspective, therefore keeping the reader privy to only the main character's knowledge and thoughts. It's an especially effective choice for writers with a strong, stylish voice.

I am First Person perspective! Everything is in relation to me, my thoughts, and what I say. I hope you like me. If not, I will try telling you even more about me!

More on this in a bit.

3) **Third Person** — Think of it as the demigod of Omniscient Voice; it has some God-like powers by allowing the author to shift points of view — but to a limited capacity. All observations, thoughts and dialogue must be linked to character perspectives. There is no external narrative and there is limited opportunity for foreshadowing. The advantage of Third Person is that it allows more exploration of characters and situations than First Person, but without the additional burden of establishing an Omniscient narrative. Think of it as Kanye West, and not just because he thinks he's a god. Third Person is like having access to lots of back-up singers to help you sound better.

I am Third Person perspective! I can do things that mortal First Person can't do! But I will never live up to the expectations of my Omniscient father!

Stop talking to yourself, TP!

*Sorry dad! *whimpers**

And finally,

4) **Last Person perspective** — The least popular and most difficult technique a writer can attempt, mostly because Last Person voice always goes something like this…

I just got here, so what did I miss? WHAT?! Why am I ALWAYS the last person to know!

Let's get back to First Person perspective now (See? I told you we would). Keep in mind that the same things that make writing from this perspective so effective in establishing a relationship with your reader can just as quickly end that relationship – for the same reason many relationships end: Too much focus on "Me," "My" and "I."

Although "not putting the toilet seat down" is a close second.

According to the word count indicator, we are nearly 500 words into this chapter. Including the references I'm about to make, the "I" or "Me" words have been used nine times. And because I know some of you are now going back to count, I'll wait here…

…Okay, fine. Ten times.

The point is, one of the easiest ways for a columnist or blogger to avoid too many "I" references is to replace them with "We" when possible. Not only do you cut down on the "I" words, but you also make the readers feel they are part of what's happening. Assuming they want to, which isn't always the case with my readers.

But you get the idea.

While this technique doesn't necessarily apply to first person novel writing, the basic methods of avoiding too many references to yourself are the same.

Let's take that last paragraph and change it to how it could have been written by using more "I" words…

> **My** point is, one of the easiest ways for **me** to avoid too many "**I**" references is by replacing them with "We" whenever **I** can. Not only do **I** cut down on the "**I**" words, but it also helps **me** make the **my** readers feel they are part of what **I'm** writing…

Ech! Have you seen paragraphs like that before? I mean, other than in the last 15 seconds? It makes you want to stop reading because the writer is talking *at* you instead of *with* you. This brings us back to the relationship analogy, and why it's important to look at your writing – whether it be a column, blog post, short story or novel – as a conversation which encourages a relationship. If you're doing all the talking, the other person will stop engaging in the conversation and, eventually, he or she will find someone else.

Probably at a book store.

So how do you avoid too many "I" references while still establishing your voice? Again, it's relationship time. Once you've written your first draft, go back over it with your reader in mind and eliminate those "I" references – either with a simple "We" fix or, if necessary, by re-working the passages to be more inclusive. That said, avoid going to the polar opposite with your revisions because, as in any a relationship, you also want to avoid losing your voice entirely.

So, let's suppose 50 pages into your *First Person* perspective manuscript you make a startling realization: You are completely sick of yourself. However, you don't want to ditch the manuscript entirely, because the story is good. It may be time to try switching to *Third Person* or *Omniscient* perspective.

At the risk of sounding politically incorrect, I think every good writer needs a certain level of multiple personality disorder. That's because, as a writer, you need to have the ability to do more than simply observe and notate things about people and situations; you have to be able to inhabit them in the same way that, say… Justin Bieber inhabits his role as a skinny Caucasian gangster.

To do this, you have to be willing – and able – to step outside yourself and experience things as someone else might, in order to formulate reactions and dialogue that ring true. Even as a columnist, I have a few fictional individuals who make appearances from time to time in my writing, because they allow me to approach some subjects more effectively than through simple narrative. One of these individuals is "Ima Knowitall," a self-proclaimed "best selling author" behind the (pretend) novel, *Fifty Shades of Time-Traveling Vampire Love*.

Confession time: I'm not actually a 30-something, pessimistic female writer who wants so much to believe in her own fame that she constantly projects a ludicrous facade of celebrity.

No, it's true.

Ima Knowitall is a character I turn to when I feel that exploring an idea is better served — and more engaging for readers — by my taking a back seat in a First Person scenario. That's where multiple personality disorder comes into play. As we discussed earlier, even if what you're writing about is an over-the-top character or situation, readers will be willing to suspend their disbelief as long as there is an element of truth. Screenwriters for sci-fi, horror and action movies constantly rely on this element to convince viewers to go along for the ride.

In order to make a character like Ima Knowitall work, three things need to happen:

1) What she says and does must stay true to her character.
2) My reactions and responses to her must embellish, not contradict her.
3) Anyone else we "interact with" must do the same.

To pull that off, we have to engage our MPDs in order to shift our points of view convincingly from one individual to the next. For novelists, this is the first step in graduating from linear, plot-driven writing to richer, character-driven stories.

Or in the case of a humor columnist, the first step toward a mandatory psychological exam.

What follows is an excerpt from one of three pieces I did on "Ima," utilizing many of the tools we've discussed. As you read through, see if you can spot them:

> … Ima Knowitall is the author of more than 40 online novels published this past year, and was recently honored by the Society of Illiterate Columnists (SIC) for her contributions to "… the advancement of people who write without the shackles of proper grammar." So meeting an author of her caliber on the eve of her latest release, 50 Shades of Time-Traveling Vampire Love, was very exciting. As Ima had mentioned before, her celebrity could get us into any number of exclusive eateries in the Los Angeles area, including a Beverly Hills country club where the chef prepares a special taco quiche every day, exclusively for her, just in case she comes to eat.

"But the paparazzi are always there waiting for me, so we'll have to go somewhere else. I'm thinking Del Taco. You drive," said Ima, who reminded me that the private bus she had arrived in, which had been cleverly "disguised as public transportation" and filled with celebrity friends "dressed incognito," wouldn't be back to pick her up until 10:05, 10:35, 11:00 or 11:20. "I have it follow a specially scheduled route so I can throw off all the autograph hounds," she explained.

The price of celebrity and its trade offs is something one must be willing to accept. I confessed to Ima that, given the choice, I wasn't sure I'd be willing to pay that price.

"Yeah… wait," she said. "You're still paying for breakfast though, right?"

We arrived at Del Taco to find it had been turned into a Bentos place called Julie's Hot Box. Clearly frustrated, Ima suggested an exclusive country club I'd never heard of called the Panting Cheetah, which was on Culver City's east side.

"Their all-day nacho bar opened at 8 a.m.," said Ima. "It's just like having tacos, except with a bunch of broken shells."

Upon entering the Panting Cheetah, it was obvious we had arrived too early because none of the staff was completely dressed yet. But being professionals, and due in large part to Ima's celebrity status, they served us anyway, and even offered us the nacho bar "compliments of the house, as long as you buy a beer."

Me: I suppose you just get used to the star treatment everywhere you go?

Ima: Yeah. Did you buy the beer yet?

Me: Yes. I gave our waitress a twenty. I'm just waiting for my change.

Ima: This isn't Applebee's. You'll be lucky to get your beer. *shovels nachos into her mouth*

Me: Let's talk about Love Vampires. Do you think it's your best novel?

Ima: Absolutely. It only took one day.
Me: It's 540 pages.
Ima: *from the nacho bar* I didn't sleep a wink all day!
Me: You describe Love Vampires as a simple story: Edwardo meets a whiny teen-aged girl named Ella. Ella realizes she likes things a little rough. Edwardo turns out to be time-traveling Mexican vampire. What was your inspiration?
Ima: I love Mexican food. *licking fingers* The rest just came to me.
Me: Let's switch gears and talk about technique. Do you outline your novels first?
Ima: As long as it fits on a square of Bugle cigarette paper. I smoke a lot. Cigarettes, too.
Me: Do you keep your notes organized somehow for future reference?
Ima: *from the nacho bar* No, I generally roll them up and smoke them.
Me: Do you base your characters on real people or are they completely fictional.
Ima: As far as I know, I've never actually met a Mexican vampire *grabs passing topless waitress by suspender* You're out of taco meat. *lets suspender snap back*

Moments later, we quickly left the Panting Cheetah to avoid what Ima said was a large, angry autograph seeker approaching our table. I dropped her off just in time to catch the return of her private bus "disguised as public transportation," which had a whole new set of celebrity passengers this time! I couldn't help but marvel at the cleverness of one, who chose to avoid drawing attention to himself by disguising himself as Pauly Shore…

Did you recognize any of the tools utilized in that passage to establish its voice?
This brings us to an important symptom of writing psychosis: *Talking to oneself.*

Let me clarify that this shouldn't occur in a room full of strangers. But when utilized as a tool in the privacy of your home or office — or even during your morning commute (I pretend to have a Bluetooth) — actually verbalizing dialogue is the best way to hear if it rings true. Not only will it identify phrasing that would be too difficult for someone to say

---

(**Note:** This does not apply to dialogue written by George Lucas), but it can also be an integral part of "inhabiting" that individual in the same way an actor verbally explores a script to understand delivery and motivation.)

That being said, there will also be times when you need to talk with someone else. I don't mean a mental health professional so much as I mean an individual similar to your character. In chapter five, we talked about how doing research adds a level of credibility that readers will relate to. It provides the details that move your readers beyond generalities and suspends them in a level of fictional reality. That kind of reality only comes from experience, and assuming you don't have time to become an Olympic athlete, airline pilot or homicide detective, your best bet is to talk with those who have.

Regardless of what you may think after reading one of my columns, one of the strangest experiences I've ever had as a writer didn't take place at the keyboard.

It actually occurred in a beauty parlor.

The woman I was interviewing was sitting under a hair dryer throughout our conversation, which meant we had to raise our voices the entire time. Naturally, this drew more than a few stares from other patrons getting perms, waxes and pedicures. While I'm sure some of the stares had to do with the fact we were practically yelling for 40 minutes, I think it had more to do with the nature of our conversation: The woman, named KK, was sharing her experiences as a homicide detective.

A lot of it wasn't pretty. But it was raw, real and included the kinds of details you can't get from simply reading *Wikipedia* articles. The smells, physical evidence, procedures that aren't "by the book," but recognized by working detectives — all of it was there, presented from the source during one of the most surreal conversations I've ever had. It's where I learned about pattern lividity, and how, in one case, the deep bruising caused by a Lone Star belt buckle was uncovered using ultraviolet light — and how, within hours, it had been confiscated from the suspect's home and matched with the bruise found on the body of his nine-year-old stepson.

As I said, it wasn't pretty.

So why was I there at that beauty shop? I mean aside from my need for a mani-pedi? I was getting background for a mystery novel. Although I knew my characters and had completed an outline, I needed the kind of details that would not only add realism and plausibility, but would be so compelling they could take the story in unexpected directions. Even as a humor columnist, I use this approach.

Whatever you're writing, your research should include talking with people:

1) Whenever your piece includes something you aren't an expert on.
2) Whenever it's possible

For a lot of writers, talking with people is like needing a cavity filled: You know it has to be done, you're sure it will be painful, and you'd be willing to fill it yourself with wood putty. But writing about characters in a way that's believable, and constructing a story that feels as if it follows a natural sequence of events — through conversation, observation and consequence — requires a working knowledge of your fictional world and those who inhabit it. To do that, you have to talk to people who have lived in the real version of it.

As always, begin with the research and educate yourself as much as possible about the subject you're fleshing out. Not only will this give you a better idea of the kinds of questions you need to be asking, but it will keep you from wasting time asking about the obvious. Remember: In most cases you'll only have one opportunity to speak with an interviewee, so make the most of it by being prepared. The person will appreciate it, and you will get more out of the talk if you've taken the time to cover the basics. If you're interviewing a chef, you don't want to waste time asking the correct temperature for meat sauce; you want to know the secret recipe.

When it comes to the actual interview, here are a few tips I've learned based on trial, error and forgetting batteries for my recorder:

> 1) *Let the interviewee pick the interview location.* You want the person to be comfortable and in a familiar element. That's where the interviewee will have his or her best recollections and be more apt to reveal details. Although my interview with KK was in a beauty shop, it was her choice — and in a place she frequented. Plus, it allowed me to get a much-needed trim. Which had nothing to do with the interview, but I'm just saying…

> 2) *Use a small recording device and avoid a pad and pen.* There are several reasons for this, aside from the fact that I can't read my own writing. Eye contact is important during an interview — for you and your subject. Making eye contact with the person you're interviewing fosters a conversational approach. Again, make your contact comfortable and you will get more out of the talk. For you, not having your eyes buried in a notepad allows you to observe body language and facial expressions — things that will come back to you when you begin writing. They also provide you with visual cues that can help lead the interview into different directions. Does the person suddenly look uncomfortable? It may be time to take a different approach — or maybe dig deeper. You'll know when you see it, but can't if you're looking into a notebook.

And last:

> 3) *Use your list of questions sparingly.* I think of them as icebreakers — something to get the conversation going or to refer to if there's a lull or dead end. Just like a great book reads well when it feels "unscripted," the same applies to a good interview. Think of it this way: Want to tour the country? Stay on the main highway. Want to get

away from the tourists and see the real America? Take the back roads and be spontaneous. That's where you'll find the people and places you'll remember most.

And so will your readers.
Assuming they can hear you over the hair dryer.

7
Take a step back

    When I was a kid, my family and I went to Mexico to help build a small, one-room medical/dental office in a poor section outside of Tijuana. My dad and I were assigned to hang doors while others were framing and running electrical wire. It was crucial that the doorways be square if we wanted to hang doors that didn't look like something out of Alice in Wonderland. But every time we got ready to hang a door, we'd re-check the frame and it would be out of square, even though it was perfect minutes earlier. After three or four times, my dad stomped off in frustration and walked to the top of a small hill overlooking the work site. Minutes later, I heard him laughing as he motioned for me to join him on the hill. Once I got there, I could see why. With everyone working at the same time on all four sides, the entire structure was swaying ever so slightly, including the door frames. Though it seemed like everything was working together, it wasn't until taking a step back that we saw why nothing was going to be square until we changed the way we were building our structure.

Writing is the same way: It's important to take a step back from time to time and look at how the overall structure is coming together. In keeping with the medical/dental office theme, here's how maintaining your story's focus and "squareness" can be a lot like a going in for a dental check-up and eye exam.

Open wide, please…

Flossing

A good dentist will tell you it's important to floss between meals, and will demonstrate its importance by flossing for you during your visit. That's unless he also happens to be your proctologist, in which case I'd like to welcome you to the new company health care plan.

As writers, we need to "floss" regularly in order to keep tarter — in the form of over-used or cliché words and descriptions — from building up in our writing. During an initial draft, particularly in novel writing, the objective is to get your thoughts, ideas and general direction down on paper. If inspiration strikes during a descriptive passage in your first draft, great! But if you're like the rest of us, and you end up with a description like "the setting sun was like a navel orange slowly descending into God's fruit basket," acknowledge it for the tarter that it is and know you will floss it out later. If you already take this approach, then give yourself a sticker.

Heck, take a pencil, too!

The problem occurs when we allow ourselves to fall into a pattern of last-minute writing and editing, leaving little or no time to floss. Unless this pattern is recognized and reversed, the tarter builds until, one day while sitting across from an editor or publisher, you open your mouth to discuss your manuscript and notice a distinct odor. At that point, discreetly flossing is no longer an option. Even with one of those little, single-use flossers I'm always finding on the ground.

Try this helpful tip: Think of the first draft as an open mouth, with one of those shoe horn-type devises jammed in there to reveal the teeth of someone who just ate Thanksgiving dinner…

Ok, so I realize that wasn't as helpful as it first seemed in my mind. The point I'm trying to make is that, no matter how unpleasant and time consuming, it's important to recognize the need for "flossing" each sentence, paragraph and page of your writing to get rid of tarter-like cliché's and reveal those pearly whites that shine with inspiration. (Did I mention Colgate is also a sponsor of this book?)

Brushing

Just as in maintaining good oral hygiene, the next step after a good flossing is brushing. In this case, it means going back over things once the "tartar" has been cleared away. That's when potential problems — gaps, looseness, or even the need for an extraction — can be recognized, while thoroughly brushing through what you've written. Use a firm brush, not a soft one. If you do it right, there should be a little "bleeding" involved as you make some tough decisions and acknowledge flaws.

If there's a lot of blood, you may consider switching genres. Possibly to horror.

Gargle and rinse

After my unfortunate "think of your first draft as an open mouth" analogy, some of you may still be sitting there, motionless, with drool pooling on your tongues. "Gargling" seemed like a good opportunity for you to take care of that before someone notices.

There is something to be said about gargling, when it comes to your manuscript, as well. Just as gargling regularly with your favorite mouth wash — Scope, Listerine, Fireball cinnamon whiskey — should be part of your daily oral hygiene ritual to maintain freshness and prevent decay, a final "gargling rinse" should follow "flossing" and "brushing" your manuscript. The truth is, things may look sparkly clean, but taking the time to give it one more rinse is a good idea.

Just be careful where you spit.

HEY! Those are my shoes!

Looks like it's time for that eye exam I promised earlier…

Check your visual acuity

We're all familiar with the Snellen chart, which is the chart you stand 20 feet away from while trying to decipher a series of letters, which, as they get smaller, begin to resemble the ingredients listed on a bag of Cheetos. The objective is to determine how far a person can get from a particular point before losing focus. The same goes for writers. In the same way a person may not realize how bad his vision has become until he's using a urinal that's actually a display refrigerator on the main floor at Sears, a writer can slowly lose a story's focus until it has become blurred by extemporaneous passages of description, too many characters, sub-plots or dialogue that don't advance the story.

How can you test to make sure your narrative vision is still clear?

Stand 20 feet away from your monitor. If you can still read it without squinting so hard it appears you're having a stroke, forget writing and become a sharpshooter. In lieu of that, follow the "20/20" rule of writing: If after reading every 20th paragraph in your story (or in the case of a short story, every 20th sentence) you still have a clear idea of what's happening, who the central characters are and the major plot points, you're writing's vision is "normal." If after several of these 20/20 paragraphs you begin to lose focus, stop and go back to where you lost sight; chances are your story began to blur somewhere between the first line and those Cheetos ingredients.

Step two

Test your peripheral vision. This is the part of the exam where your optometrist tells you to keep looking ahead while he moves an object from behind you toward the front of your head, at which point you're supposed to acknowledge when you see it in your peripheral vision. FYI, this is also when your optometrist stands behind you and makes faces or plays air guitar without you knowing it. Regardless, having good peripheral vision is important for writers, too. Your "writing peripherals" are those things that run parallel to the main action and include expendable characters, foreshadowing and some unanticipated secondary themes that develop through character interaction and plot development. This is all good stuff, because, if done well, these elements can add a sense of immediacy, spontaneity and unpredictability that keep readers invested in the story.

However, just like that optometrist playing air guitar behind your back, it's easy to lose sight of what's going on if you don't keep your peripherals in check. In optometry, the ideal measurement is at least 70 degrees of vision in the horizontal meridian. From a writing standpoint, this means the peripheral elements of your story shouldn't account for more than about 30 percent of your story development. Put another way: If you've written 70 pages and more than 30 of them revolve around the actions of secondary characters, themes or developments not directly related to your main characters, they are just playing air guitar. It's time to re-evaluate the focus of your story, and whether the secondary characters/themes are becoming blurred with the main plot and characters.

Step three

Check for depth perception. Optometrists often check for this by tossing something at the patient, such as a Nerf ball, to determine binocular (two-eye) vision, which allows us to see in three dimensions. As a kid, I thought I had monocular vision because of how horrible I was at dodge ball. After a visit to my optometrist I was relieved to find out I was just really uncoordinated. In terms of writing, a 3D world is also important, although not having it won't lead to bruising. Unfortunately, unlike the previous steps, there is no real "formula" to determine if you have created a three-dimensional world in your writing. What I can tell you as that, as writers, we tend to fill in the blanks ourselves and, as a result, it's easy to envision more on the page than is actually there.

So how can you see if your writing vision has depth? Take a chapter and eliminate all the dialogue. Then read it or, better yet, read it *to* someone. The objective has nothing to do with plot or character; it's about whether or not your descriptive vision has made it onto the page. When you're done, have the person describe what came across. If it resembles what you envisioned, chances are you're writing in three dimensions! If the person can't describe things clearly, then throw something at them.

Or better yet, go back to your manuscript and figure out how to make your vision clearer in the next draft.

8
Do you feel a draft?

    Whether writing a 500-word column or 400-page manuscript, there comes that satisfying moment when you hit the final keystroke. The sound echoes, in slow motion, reverberating through your body and outward, catching anyone within a three-mile radius in its ripple effect. Outside your window, traffic comes to a stop. Drivers and pedestrians join together, taking time from their day to cheer, launch balloons, lay bouquets and luminarias at your doorstep, and applaud so hard their hands turn red.
    And wait — is that a tear I see glistening in the eye of the Fed-Ex driver? It's embarrassing, really.
    But who can blame them? Your own brilliance is looking back at you from the monitor! How clever you are!
    Especially that line about how being a parent is like training donkeys, and there are thymes when your children just need a swift kick in the…

Hold. The. Phone.

"Thymes?!"

This brings us to the next moment following that final keystroke, when the applause subsides, and you suddenly notice that the cleverness looking back at you from your screen is spelled "cleaverness."

Is that a draft you feel on your exposed backside?

Yes, it is. And, depending on the size of your manuscript and how much time you have — and whether you've gotten up and closed the window — it should only be the first of three drafts you'll need to complete before submitting your piece for publication. Which isn't to say you can't do more than three. In fact, when it comes to book manuscripts, expect *at least* three drafts before you can, once and for all, be asked by your publisher to change your story from third-person to first-person in order to add a sense of immediacy.

At which point you will, with total immediacy, seriously consider a job in public sanitation.

But let's suppose the head of public works tells you, in no uncertain terms, that things are backed up in the sanitation department. And let's suppose you manage to keep a straight face long enough to return to your computer and continue pursuing a writing career.

In that case, it's time to start the next draft of your manuscript.

In addition to being a columnist, I'm also a volunteer firefighter. When you get down to it, putting out a structure fire is also a three-draft process:

Initial Attack

Overhaul

Clean-up

I've adopted these firefighting terms for the three phases of my writing and editing routine. Not only because I think they accurately describe each phase, but also because they sound way cooler than:

Draft one

Draft two

Draft (yawwwn) …

See what I mean?

The *Initial Attack* phase is exactly what it sounds like: You have assembled what you need, know your plan of action and are on-scene with your nozzle wide open, flooding the page with your ideas in a steady stream without interruption.

Great. Now I have to use the restroom…

Thanks for waiting.

The Initial Attack is when you don't worry about spelling, punctuation or other grammatical concerns that will slow down your progress in getting thoughts and ideas on the page.

The Initial Attack is what writers — and firefighters — live for.

Next comes the not-so-fun, but equally important, phase of the draft process: *Overhaul*.

This is when you take a deep breath and look around to see what the fire has done, what dangers remain, and take care of anything that could flare up again later. As a writer, the same rules apply. Take a look at your pages as if they're rooms in a house. And if your house has 400 rooms, the IRS is looking forward to your manuscript.

Go through each page, line by line, and look for obvious errors — typos, misspelling, run-on sentences, improper tense changes, etc. As you do, keep a red pen handy to keep notes. I often get additional ideas, or think of better phrasing, as I go through this process. Write them down and refer to them by page and paragraph so, when you go back, you can address them easily.

Once you've made your grammar corrections and implemented your revisions, take a break and clear your head.

On a fire scene, it's easy to get tunnel vision after a while. Especially if you're extinguishing a car fire inside an actual tunnel. The same thing can happen during the draft process as a writer. So give yourself 30 minutes or so to get a fresh set of eyes before beginning the final phase: *Clean-up*. (BTW, Stephen King takes a break of three months before tackling the final read through of any novel he writes! See *On Writing*, by King.)

At this point, you've gone through everything twice, corrected the grammatical "dangers" you discovered during Overhaul, and have made revisions to your manuscript that improve upon the original draft.

Clean-up is that final walk-through you give before telling residents — or publishers — "Hey, everything has been done to make sure you won't get burned."

Read through this draft out loud. If you can arrange to have it read back to you by someone else, such as Morgan Freeman, even better! Hearing your words read by someone else can reveal awkward phrasing your mind skips over because IT knows what you're trying to say; someone else may not.

Regardless, read through it twice: once aloud and once to yourself. If you don't find any "hot" spots, it's time to clear the scene and secure your manuscript for publication.

If not, another draft is still in order.

I'm sure it goes without saying, but I'd like to clarify when I say "three-draft" process, I'm not talking about how many beers it takes to loosen up those typing fingers. I'm talking about the *minimum* number of drafts you should make of your story or manuscript before you push the "publish" or email button. That said, I'm not suggesting you can't do *more* than three, if that's what it takes to make your manuscript the best it can be. At the same time, avoid allowing yourself to get stuck in an endless cycle of revisions. If you're on the 20th draft of a five-paged short story you've been revising for the last three years, it's time to ask yourself if you might be purposely stalling.

I recently had a conversation with a blogger who is an aspiring writer. She confessed to having a 100-paged "work in progress" she's been revising on a weekly basis for six years. Her plan is to make it available online as a self-published novella. When asked when she thought it would be done, she wasn't sure.

"I think it's time to consider forced labor," I told her. "This baby is so overdue that, if it were a child, it would come out eating solid foods."

[**Official Disclaimer:** I am not an actual doctor, although I have played one. Just not on TV. *cough cough*]

Inevitably, she realized she was stalling out of fear of failure; as long as her novella remained unpublished — and unread — the hope it would be a "big success" remained. As I've mentioned, "success" is a relative term. The only failed writing project is the one that is never started. If you've completed one or more drafts of your manuscript, then you're already a success, because you've beaten the odds by doing something many people talk about but never attempt — let alone finish. Think of it as making the world's best submarine sandwich; whether or not anyone takes a bite, it's still a great sandwich. Having others walk around with mustard stains on their shirts is just a bonus.

So, if you're carrying around a nine-pound, fully-developed manuscript, ask yourself what you're truly waiting for and why. Be honest with your answer. Don't let fear of failure keep your literary baby from entering the world.

Chances are, it's time to start *pushing* for a delivery. *wink wink*

9
A word on endings

Readers can tell when you're searching for an ending, which is a little like watching a gambler rolling the dice one more time to recoup his losses, or a wife knowing her husband has no idea where he's driving, regardless of how many times he says he knows the way. As a writer, you have to be able to recognize when this is happening and either cut your losses or ask for directions, when it comes to a satisfying ending to your manuscript.

By cutting your losses, I don't mean tossing everything into a backyard fire pit and dancing around the flames in nothing but body paint as your neighbors threaten to call the police. I mean start at the end of what you've written and work backwards. This is a variation of a technique used by some abstract artists, who will look into a mirror at their painting to get a different perspective and spark ideas. In writing, it can reveal patterns and redundancies, which, if you trace them to the beginning, often point to where you need to end.

(**Warning:** Do not hold your monitor up to a mirror and read it backwards. It will only give you a headache.)

If that sounds too cumbersome, consider asking for directions. What I mean is exactly that: Have someone read what you have written and ask that person for some direction. You'd be surprised how insightful your local gas station attendant can be. If you don't feel like driving, or are worried about getting lost, ask a family member, fellow blogger, or neighbor; it doesn't have to be a writer or English major. More than likely, the problem is that you're over analyzing. The last thing you need is more deep analysis; you just want a fresh set of eyes.

If you suspect your neighbor has a fresh set of eyes in the refrigerator, then a trip to the gas station might be safer.

Hopefully, writers' groups are also a potential source for feedback and direction. I have several blogger friends who are heavily involved in their local writer' groups. They receive constructive feedback and continued support from their fellow writers on a regular basis. Clearly, collaborating openly with other writers on a regular basis can be beneficial. Especially if everyone pitches in for appetizers and wine.

But be careful. I have been involved in a few writers' groups over the years, from Atlanta, Ga. to Portland, Ore. My experience — based on the five or six I have attended — has been hit-and-miss. Each time, I went in with an open mind, anticipating of a true exchange of ideas and constructive feedback. And on three different occasions, I found myself sneaking out the back door on my hands and knees under a veil of cigarette and pipe smoke. In each of those instances, one or more of the following writers group members were present:

Be Honest, But Only If It Means I'm Brilliant

These people always arrive early enough to explain their brilliance ahead of time, thus ensuring everyone agrees with their brilliance before they read their work — which is usually five to 10 pages beyond the allotted amount. But who cares when it's that brilliant! Once these members are finished reading, they sit back with satisfaction, look into the confused expressions of their listeners and say, "Please be honest — what did you think?" They don't ask this question because they really want to hear constructive criticism; they ask because they are expecting praise. Nothing more. They don't want collaboration; they want validation. These writers will never expand their skills because they are more concerned with rationalizing their brilliance than they are with learning how to wield the tools needed to actually be brilliant.

Plus they usually drink all the wine.

I'd Rather Offer Excuses For My Writing Than Set Expectations

These writers are the first to criticize their work, usually upon arrival. Though they have the least amount of pages to read aloud, it takes twice as long because they also offer a running commentary on why it's terrible — sort of like Mystery Science Theater 3000, with the critic sitting in the front row pointing out how the space ship looks more like a flying bed pan. In the same way that being blind to your shortcomings is detrimental to your growth as a writer, so is having a need to make sure you point out your faults before anyone else can. Again, like "Brilliant" writers, "Excuses" writers stop growing because they are so busy being the first to identify their own failures that they completely overlook those times when their work is actually pretty brilliant.

Plus, they almost always drop something into the cheese dip.

Everyone's Writing Is Super Fantastic

For obvious reasons, these members are the "Brilliant" writers' favorite critics. That's because whether you are reading a passage from Steinbeck or the ingredients from a box of Kraft Macaroni and Cheese, these people will say things like, "Marvelous!" or "Look at my goosebumps!" or "Someone get my agent!" when in fact what they are really thinking is, "I should probably get more wine before that blowhard who thinks he's so brilliant drinks it all." The "Super Fantastic" writers tend to see a writers group as a social activity. They take praise and criticism equally well because, let's face it: they don't take either very seriously.

Plus, since the Bunko group disbanded, they're just glad to have a place to go on Sunday nights.

And last,

My Completed Manuscript Means I'm Better

In most cases, these members' 1,100-page manuscripts have been complete for at least three years — which, coincidentally, happens to be how long it's been since they started the group. These members have yet to submit their manuscripts to anyone and are forever in the "final draft" phase, because actually submitting their work would mean risking rejection. They are content with their on-going identity as the group's potential best selling authors. In truth, their writing growth stopped the moment the final key was tapped on their novels.

Plus, they never have their own highlighter.

So, does this mean I don't encourage joining a writers' group? Not at all. As I said, collaborating with — and seeking feedback from — fellow writers can be a terrific experience that not only fosters your development, but weaves a support network for yourself and others.

But if you join a group and recognize one or more of the members I've mentioned, remember to stay low.

I'll meet you outside.

Writing is like flying:
Magical.
With some turbulence.

10
Are we there yet?

A finished manuscript is just the beginning. At least it is if you want your work to be published, either on your own through self publication or with a publishing house. This chapter is about what to expect during that process, how to keep perspective when things don't go as planned, and how to hold onto your identity as a writer even when you feel it's in question.

For me, the best analogy for what a writer goes through from manuscript to publication is ski jumping. Years ago, I attempted to ski jump using a pair of roller skates and our children's backyard slide. I'm not going to get into the details, other than to say there was a fair amount of screaming (from me, not the kids), not much "hang time" and a nearly fatal touch-down, which was technically more of an Olympic-sized face-plant. The feelings evoked by that memory are similar to those I have experienced many times during my writing career.

Writing, like ski jumping, starts at the top of the slope. Just like a ski jumper looking out over the expanse of winter-blanketed hills, all writers experience that inspired moment when they find themselves at a literary vista; a story or novel idea suddenly materializes before them and it is breathtaking and full of possibilities.

Then, as with ski jumpers, once the magnitude of what they are about to embark on settles in, there is a sudden moment of panic as they question the logic of what they're doing. Or at the very least, whether they should've used the restroom before getting sealed into that polymer jumpsuit. For this reason, I stopped wearing a polymer jumpsuit while writing.

Next, they get into position.

This is when a writer commits to the jump. There is no turning back at this point. In most cases, it's because the writer or ski jumper is too driven — by the possibilities and potential — to step away from the jumping-off point. In most cases, there is someone standing behind them, such as a coach, publisher or agent, offering encouragement and support. Sometimes while holding a cattle prod.

Then suddenly, it's time to go down the slope!

This is when a jumper or writer gains momentum while battling resistance through a combination of fortitude and technique. This portion of the jump is the most critical because its execution will dictate how far the person will fly and how successful the landing will be. Trust me, as the aluminum foil winner of the backyard roller skate jump, I can tell you that poor execution at this point can lead to disappointment.

And hundreds of views on YouTube.

For a writer, this is a time of mixed emotions like *exhilaration* (This is going to be AWESOME!), *second guesses* (Should I have gone to trade school?), and *self-realization* (I think I'm going to be sick). For a ski jumper, it's time to clear the mind of everything but a single thought: *STOP! STOP! STOP!*

Then, WHOOSH! He leaves the end of the jump shoot!

This is when the true leap of faith comes into play, figuratively and literally, depending on your level of health care coverage. All the preparation — the endless revisions, the constant adjustments in phrasing, the countless hours of re-writing — all have led to this moment, as you take to the air and once again survey the literary vista! You lean forward, tuck your arms to your sides and hold your breath, hoping to remain suspended and within full view of the world for as long as possible!

Then reality sets in: *I still have to LAND this thing!*

At first glance (assuming you had your eyes open during the jump), the landing appears to be the end. It's the part where you return to Earth and touch down gracefully before sliding to a stop in front of the Outback Steakhouse banner. Friends and family are there to applaud you as you look back to the judges and see how well you scored!

The. End.

Right?

Not exactly. The landing is just another beginning, in many ways. If you executed well in the air, it makes the landing more successful, but, like an Olympic ski jumper, the work continues in order to build on that last jump — so that you can fly higher, go farther and avoid that leg cramp next time. In other words, just because you've struck the landing doesn't it's time to stop waxing your skis. It just means it's time to get more wax.

The only exception to this is if you are attempting a second run on the backyard slide jump, in which case wax is a really bad idea.

Trust me, I know.

Speaking of face planting in your children's empty kiddie pool, let's talk a little about what to expect if you're going to shop your manuscript around to publishers. In my opinion, every writer should attempt to find a publisher first, even if you're pretty sure you're are going to self-publish. The reason is simple: Other than time, postage and a potential rejection letter, you have nothing to lose and everything to gain. Give yourself a time period — say six months — to find a publisher. Do your research and narrow your submissions to six publishers who you feel could be a good fit for you. Base this determination on:

The kinds of books they publish (Do they include your genre?)

The types of authors they represent (Do you know and/or like their work?)

If they publish first-time authors (Some only work with established authors and agents, so it's their loss.)

If they work hands-on with their writers (For your first book, you want that kind of support.)

What your gut tells you (It's like house hunting; you know if a place feels right or not.)

Six months, six publishers and five questions. Mostly because one more question would make this a really bad number.

So let's suppose you've spent time searching the Internet for potential publishers and, after many hours of watching cat videos, you've also decided on six (publishers, not cats.) Now it's time to query them.

In 2002, I began my unofficial "Internet promotional tour" across the United States by emailing a basic cover letter and links to a few sample columns to newspapers here in my home state of Oregon. Today, the column is running in 40 papers in 11 states and Canada. Here are a few suggestions to help distinguish your email query from the hundreds of male enhancement offers publishers receive each day.

However, before we get to that, I want you to keep a couple of things in mind. First, in the same way that emailing your query makes things faster and easier for you, it's also faster and easier for publishers to delete your submission without ever reading it. I'm sorry, but that's just part of the trade off.

What you gain, of course, is more queries in less time, without the expensive postage.

Why wait weeks for rejection when you can have it within hours at no extra cost?!?

Which brings me to my second point: Developing a tough skin isn't nearly as important as keeping a clear perspective on things. The fact is, even the best query can go unopened by a prospective publisher. Going through long periods without a response shouldn't be taken as a reflection of your writing ability. Neither is getting multiple rejections.

However, multiple rejections written in ALL-CAPS could be cause for concern.

Hopefully by this point in the book you're saying to yourself, (a) Ned might actually have some useful information, or (b) I think I remember deleting his query letter. Either way, we're ready to begin talking about the specifics of formatting your email query.

Create a cover letter:

Your letter should be limited to a single page, shorter if possible. If it can be summarized using only bar code, all the better. Just make sure it includes three things: 1) a simple introduction, 2) why you are querying and, 3) any information that gives your work merit, such as any writing awards, previous publication credits or, if you're just starting out, a complimentary lottery scratch-it sequence potentially worth millions.

In the upper left corner, include the editor's full name, the publishing house name, and general mailing address.

For example:

Ima Cranky, Acquisitions Editor
Missing Pages Publishing
Spuds, ID

This will make your query seem less like spam or a mass mailing and improve the chances of it being read. Next, in the actual greeting, use the publisher or editor's first name.

In this case: *Dear Ima,*

You've already addressed them by full name and title in the upper left corner. There's no harm in personalizing it a bit in your greeting. If that annoys them, chances are they aren't going to be fun to work with, anyway.

Finally, close your letter the way you opened it — on a first-name basis:

I look forward to receiving your rejection letter.
Sincerely,
Ned

Below that, put your full name, general address, phone number and, if you have one, a blog or website link address:

Ned Hickson
1234 Fifth St. *And yeah, that's a fifth…not a street!*
Florence, OR 97439
541-234-5678
www.nedhickson.com

Once you've created your cover letter, save it in your email "drafts" folder. That way, when you're sending out queries, you can just copy and paste the main contents of your letter to each publisher.

NOTE: Whatever you do, *don't forget to change the name and greeting*. I once spent an entire afternoon emailing queries to newspaper editors all over Rhode Island only to discover I had forgotten to change the name. For a short period, there was a rumor going around that every editor on Rhode Island was named Biff Rogaine.

Include samples of your work:

No one opens unsolicited attachments anymore, so don't bother including any with your email query. The best way to get your work in front of a publisher is to include a link that directs them to your website or specific work you'd like them to read. A link can also include a bio page, awards page, etc. My suggestion, however, is to stick with no more than two links. If they want to know more about you, they'll do an online court records search.

Do publishers really give a [TWEET] about your social media presence?

On the surface, the advantages of establishing a blog and linking it to social media outlets like Facebook, Twitter, Tumbler, and others seems pretty obvious. The bigger your presence in the cyberworld and the larger your following, the more likely your book will catch on and be embraced in the world that truly counts: the buying world. Keep in mind, particularly for writers without a previous track record, a large online readership can get a publisher or agent to at least raise an eyebrow after reading a well-written query letter or email about your book — which is why I suggest including links to your blog or other social media sites in your email query.

That said, publishers also know that pushing the "like" or "follow" button has become a conditioned response. In short: Having 8,000 followers does not translate into 8,000 book sales.

Still, there's another "plus" to building an online presence that can be especially encouraging to an agent or publisher (and yes, the rules I am stating apply to approaching agents as well). While having a large readership may not be a true measure of the number of actual devoted readers you have, the quality of your writing and regularity in which you post will speak for itself. Notice I didn't say "frequency" with which you post. An agent or publisher isn't as interested in how often you publish as they are in your adherence to posting quality work on a regular basis.

(Disclaimer: My blog is an obvious exception to this rule.)

The dreaded "subject" box:

I've experimented with several options, including "Desperately Seeking a Benefactor," "Congrats on the Promotion," and "This Isn't a Viagra Ad." I eventually settled on "Humor Column Query."

Editors will appreciate your being up front with your subject title and, as a result, will be more likely to take a look.

Find the right person to contact:

When you get to a publisher's website, find the *Contact* or *About* link. From there, you can generally find your way to the staff directory and the appropriate editor for your genre or subject. Click the name, paste your cover letter into the text box, change the appropriate information — double check your info — and push "send." Or, you can copy/paste the email address into the window of your own email service and then do the same. But in most cases, editors are more willing to open something from their own email service than from a stranger.

That's it!

Querying your manuscript over the Internet is a lot like playing the slot machines: most of the time you're going to come up empty, but as long as you don't run out of quarters — or in this case, persistence — odds are you'll hit the jackpot from time to time.

Keep in mind that finding a publisher is a lot like trick-or-treating. Though you know there are many other writers roaming the streets, going from publishing house to publishing house, vying for the same candy, you go anyway because you know *you're special*. When a publisher comes to the door with a handful of Tums, because the real candy was handed out already, and asks, "Who are you supposed to be?", we don't let that discourage us, because we know the next house could be handing out king-sized Snickers bars. Or that Mrs. Hollins might answer the door dressed in her Cat Woman costume. As writers, we must remain optimistic by remembering to enjoy the process — not just the end result. When we were kids, deciding on our costumes and finding all the right components was as exciting as taking that first step out the door on Halloween night. Even if your vampire fangs immediately filled with drool and felt like you were wearing someone else's dentures, there was no stopping the excitement of transforming yourself into something of your own creation and offering it to the world.

We do the same as writers every time we push the "post" button or send an article, query letter or manuscript to a publisher or agent. We take what we have transformed from a blank screen or sheet of paper into something of our own creation and offer it to the world. Then, too often, we set our sights on the candy instead of taking time to enjoy what we have created as we take that first step outside. Just like the excitement we felt as kids each time we left one house and headed down the sidewalk to the next, we need to take time to revel in the anticipation and what we have created.

11
Technically speaking

    I'm just going to come out and say it: This is going to be the most boring chapter in this book.
    I mean that.
    At least I hope it is. Because if there's a topic I've covered so far that's more boring than contract language, then I really…
    HEY! Wake up!
    See what I mean?
    As sleep-inducing as this subject may be, I want you to have a basic knowledge of terms you will encounter in the event you find yourself staring blankly at a publishing contract like I did with *Humor at the Speed of Life*. After 14 years as a syndicated columnist, it was my first venture into book publishing. I remember sitting at my desk with a cup of coffee, looking at the contract, and seeing things in all-caps like "AUTHOR," "GUARANTEE" and "WARRANTS."

In my experience, the word "warrant" has never led to anything good.

Though it was a small publishing company (Port Hole Publishing, which published this book as well), I knew it had been around for 40 years as a book seller and publisher. It kept up with the times, avoiding the temptation of becoming a "vanity" press by only publishing authors it actively seeks out. Its distribution channels reach well beyond Oregon to the global market, including Canada, the United Kingdom, New Zealand, Japan, Germany, France, Australia, Alabama and many other foreign countries with a lot of consonants. It worked through a network of 25,000 retailers and 70,000 independent booksellers, not to mention all the major Internet sites like Amazon, Barnes & Noble, etc.

Sounds great!

Uhh... but what does all that *mean* exactly?

And what about legal terms like "Subsidiary Rites," "Future Book Options," "Grant of Rights" and "Royalties?"

And why are they in ALL-CAPS!

As a journalist, I am trained to recognize subtle signs like these as meaning something important.

I should explain that I had no illusions of selling so many copies that I could leave my job and, with a little planning and a commitment to eat nothing but Costco corn dogs, live off royalties for the rest of my life. Nor did I expect to reach the *New York Times Best Seller* list; if someone who reads the *New York Times* actually bought my book, that was close enough for me. In fact, my expectation for that book was very simple: Expand my readership beyond the newspaper page.

That said, let's go through the first few sections of the contract's TERMS of AGREEMENT, beginning with the Grant of Rights.

As a columnist, I have granted newspapers that carry my column "First-Time" rights, meaning that after my column is published, the rights to each revert back to me exclusively. That's pretty standard in newspaper and magazine publication. However, in this case, the publisher is asking for Exclusive Rights in terms of the book's future sales, reprint rights and subsidiary rights. What that basically means is that, while the columns are mine, the book – including any electronic rights, motion picture rights (as if), foreign translation (that's you, Alabama), serialization, re-print rights, etc. — will forever belong to the publishing company, so long as those spin-offs are in effect with the company.

I'm OK with that. If it had been a different kind of book with movie or series potential, I may have been less inclined to agree with the terms and ask for a revision.

The next section is "Author Guarantees and Warrants." Basically, this section is asking me to guarantee that the manuscript was written exclusively by me, and doesn't include anything libelous or unlawful in its content.

...Well, assuming that neither Justin Bieber or anyone from the Kardashian family will ever read it?

Sure, we're good there.

And as far as the content being written exclusively by me: Who else would willingly claim to have written that stuff?

Again, we were good.

It gets a little more tricky when we talk about "Royalties," "Future Options" and "Permissions."

Though Royalties probably doesn't need much explaining, I'll cover it anyway just to be thorough. As you know, England has a Monarchy wherein one family, known as *Royalty*, pretends to run the country while not having any actual say in anything whatsoever. From time to time, someone from the *Royal Family* comes to the U.S., and those within the publishing industry get a piece of the financial pie by writing about them.

Book royalties work in a similar way; the more excited people get about your book, the better the chance of it leaving the U.S., providing you with a piece of the financial pie while having no actual say whatsoever. The percentage of your royalties — or slice of the pie — from each book sale is determined ahead of time and agreed upon with your signature on the contract.

Generally, the percentage you receive will increase a few points with every 15,000 copies or so.

You should also receive a *Royalty Report* every six months, letting you know where all the members of the Royal Family are and how much pie they are bringing you.

This brings us to *Future Options*, which is basically a publisher's chance to get a jump on other publishers when it comes to your next book. My agreement did not include a demand from my publisher for first dibs on any sequel to *Humor at the Speed of Life*, which would likely go to pay for lawsuits brought on by Justin Bieber and the Kardashians, anyway.

Future or *First Option* rights is something generally reserved for authors of a series, such as *Harry Potter*, *Hunger Games* or *Swifties: The Many Short-Term Relationships of Taylor Swift*. However, if you think you have a hot property that is a series, think hard before entering into what could be a long-term relationship with a publisher.

Last, we have *Permissions*. This can get a little tricky because it permits the publisher to allow selections of your book to be printed in digests, abridgments, serializations, etc., without compensation to you, IF the publisher deems that it will benefit the overall sale of the book.

There is a level of trust implied here, so be careful before signing off on that.

As long as your publisher isn't making money off of providing bits from your book to be printed elsewhere (while you make nothing), giving those permissions is reasonable, and is likely a legitimate strategy to increase book sales through "teasers," breathe easy.

But if you suddenly notice 1) your publisher has a new boat in his or her driveway, and 2) you're beginning to see portions of your book in *Reader's Digest*, and 3) you hear a dramatic reading of chapter 5 by Meryl Streep on Amazon Audio Books, you may not have read your contract as well as you should have.

As I sat there looking at my contract, I can say I felt comfortable with signing. And not just because I was sitting in a massage chair. My decision to publish with Port Hole Publishing for that book and this one took place over the course of several months, with several meetings and phone conversations, and plenty of time to look over what I was signing. I not only like and respect my publisher, but am convinced she has my — as well as her company's — best interests in mind.

Both are important factors to consider in determining whether to sign that contract.

And thanks for staying awake.

(**Note from Publisher**: Mr. Hickson's explanation of contracts is not to be construed as legal advice. The opinions expressed herein are solely his own and do not represent Port Hole Publishing. But, THANKS, NED, for the vote of confidence! All-caps intended.)

12

Finding the good in rejection

I began learning how to deal with rejection as early as the second grade. That's when, in an attempt to win the affections of Mary Avioni, I ate a handful of chalk dust. My coolness factor lasted approximately 2.5 seconds: the time it took for my stomach to send everything – including my morning snack of Lorna Doones and milk – back out with enough force to reach Mary Avioni's desk from six feet away.

Needless to say, things didn't work out for Mary and me.

The following year, the arrival of a pretty Spanish girl named Zobada Sanchez inspired me to win her affection with a plan that had almost no chance of initiating my gag reflex.

I would win her over with my athletic prowess.

Reliving the details is still a little painful. I can tell you it was the best tether-ball performance of my elementary school career. I can tell you I was a dominant force, delivering a thunderous game-winning blow so loud it could ALMOST be heard over the crowd of third-grade spectators, all of whom began screaming after witnessing my nose relocated to the back of my head when I was hit by my own kill shot. A special counselor was brought in to help my classmates deal with their trauma. Meanwhile, I was lying in the nurse's office with a nose roughly the size of a manatee, realizing I had set myself up for rejection once again.

Mercifully, God intervened the next day when Billy Guthery barfed in the cafeteria on "Succotash" day — a sight that eclipsed my historic face plant.

When I fell for Sarah Getlost in the fourth grade, I was taking no chances. My father explained to me that women couldn't resist a man in uniform. He told me this while wearing a white T-shirt, Bermuda shorts and drinking a beer, so I had to take his word for it. My plan was to wait for our little league candy sale and go to her house dressed in my new baseball uniform.

In theory, it was a good plan.

In reality, Sarah Getlost answered the door wearing her new cheerleader outfit, effectively neutralizing me. So, to impress her, I gave her my candy, a new baseball and all of my money. Although I wasn't immediately rejected, it came swiftly once my mother found out and forced me to return to Sarah's house to ask for all my stuff back. I don't remember exactly what I said, only that it was awkward and involved a lot of gulping to keep the bitter taste of rejection from coming back up.

Although I think all that chalk I swallowed in the second grade helped a little.

Rejection is a part of life, particularly for writers. We set ourselves up for potential rejection every time we send out a query, have an article published online or in print, or post something to our blog or social media page. Thanks to the digital age, we have more ways than ever to receive rejection!

Something else writers have in common is that each of us has to get started the same way: By putting ourselves out there. That means we must be prepared to deal with — and learn from — the "Sara Getlost" moments in our literary world.

I'd like to share a few passages from the many rejection letters I've received over the years:

"You are a gifted wordsmith. Try somewhere else." (Were they saying I was overqualified?)

"We don't publish new authors." (If all publishing houses felt that way, there wouldn't be any new material since The Book of Genesis)

"We were close to accepting your submission but decided to pass. Good luck." (That made me feel so much better. Like that time I got that HILARIOUS winning lottery ticket that was fake.)

"Very good. Keep trying." (With what? Better stationary?)

"As Mr. Hefner's attorney, I've been asked to order you to stop writing the girls. You're only 14 and it's creepy." (Oops! Wrong kind of rejection letter.)

I have a cabinet drawer at work full of rejection letters from newspaper editors and publishing houses. Many are for my column when I was first starting out. Others are in response to a murder mystery I wrote back in the late 1990s.

And one is from Miss October 1978.

In spite of the negative connotation a rejection letter conjures up in the mind of most authors — fine, *every* author — don't overlook the more important aspects of what it represents.

To begin with, it means you've completed a written work. No number of rejection letters changes that. Regardless of whether it's a 400-page novel or a 17-syllable haiku, you have honed and polished your words to the point you are ready to send them out to the world, either in the form of sample chapters, a query, or by pushing the "publish" button on your blog or website. And make no mistake: The "comments" section on your social media site is just another form of "acceptance" or "rejection" notices.

It's also important to remember that actually receiving a rejection letter, by email or otherwise, means an editor or publisher thought enough of your work to take the time to respond. Even if it's a letter saying "No thanks, we've already committed to publishing a book on Hobbit erotica, but keep shopping this around," it says something about your writing ability. And maybe the need for professional help – and I don't mean from an agent.

Bottom line: Most editors and publishers are like us, overworked and understaffed. Sending a letter or email takes time and effort. It's more than just a rejection; it's also a compliment.

Occasionally, you may even receive some suggestions or advice in your rejection letters, such as "Blowing up the world and having everyone die at the end seemed excessive. I'd suggest finding a more satisfying end to your children's book." Keep in mind that I'm not saying you have to agree with any suggestions you're given. Hey, it's your novel, short story or magazine article, and you will always reserve the right to have the final word on how it appears in print. I'm just pointing out that if an editor or publisher was engaged enough in your submission to offer some insight, it's quite a compliment. On that same note, if you keep receiving the same suggestion from different publishers, be willing to at least consider the idea of having "Sally" and "Stubs the Legless Gopher" steal a rocket and depart from Earth before it is reduced to space dust.

Finally, don't discard your rejection letters. Keep them somewhere safe as a reminder of your commitment as a writer – and eventually as testimony to what it took to get to where you are. As a father, I've shown all my kids my rejection file at some point: when they didn't make the team; when they were turned down for the dance; when they didn't get the grade they expected; when I go on a crying jag about why my mystery novel still hasn't been published …)

We've all heard the saying that you can't get to where you're going unless you know where you came from. Or maybe I just made that up. Regardless, rejection letters are as much an indicator of that journey as seeing your work in print. They mean you have sacrificed, persevered and believed in yourself. Possibly even threatened to run over an editor or two.

(In that event, you might get rid of those letters. Just in case.)

As I mentioned, rejection for writers can come from more places than ever, thanks to the digital age. Though I've focused mostly on dealing with rejection from publishing houses or editors, in regard to submitting manuscripts or articles, I want to take a few minutes to talk about dealing with some of the rejection and negativity writers can face online as well, particularly those of us with blogs. I have several friends who have encountered hostile and even threatening comments following a post.

If you're thinking this isn't something I deal with because I'm a humor columnist, you're wrong.

I once wrote a column titled, "Tips to combat FDAD (Fruitcake Disposal Anxiety Disorder)."

Admittedly, I picked on fruitcake a little.

OK, maybe a lot.

Here's a sample…

> "…Recent studies show that mild depression after the holidays is not only common but, in many cases, the result of FDAD – Fruitcake Disposal Anxiety Disorder. On one hand, your fruitcake was a gift and therefore deserving of some measure of appreciation. On the other hand, it has already become a chew toy for the neighbor's pit bull. This often leads to feelings of anxiety long after the holidays have ended, particularly when you see 'Buster,' still intoxicated with rum, struggling to dislodge the sugar loaf from his tightly-clenched jaws. So, as a service to our readers, we are offering the following self-help guide: I'm OK– You're OK. But Give Me a Fruitcake and I'll Kill You…"

Too strong?

Some people thought so.

In fact, in my 16 years as a columnist, I received more emails and letters (yes, actual handwritten words on parchment and mailed) about this column than any other. In addition, I even had people send me fruitcake in an effort to change my mind. Granted, some of it arrived through my office window, but there was no denying I had struck a nerve with a part of my readership that was potentially still intoxicated with rum.

Here's an actual excerpt from one letter:

> "Ned Hickson: MILLIONS of people LOVE fruitcake to eat each year! We get sick of the idiotic remarks made by A@#HOLES like you! I wish you would just SHUT UP!"

The letter goes on, but you get the idea.
How did I respond?
I hung it on my wall, where it serves as a daily reminder of how, as a humor columnist, I have an obligation to avoid Boca Raton, Fla.
Actually, Gaylesville, Alabama isn't on my short list of vacation destinations either, thanks to an email I received regarding a column I wrote called "Want to get out of jury duty? Wear a tinfoil hat." In it, I talked about how frivolous lawsuits are souring people on the judicial process and undermining the importance of jury duty. The following excerpt apparently angered one Alabama woman to the point she hopes to be a jurist if I'm ever on trial in her state. I'm currently checking to make sure I don't have any warrants pending in Alabama. Here's the part that prompted her angry email…

> "…Admittedly, I once found myself driving down the road with an 800-degree onion ring searing my flesh. I had just left a fast food drive-through and, after maintaining my composure long enough to exit the parking lot, pounced on my combo meal like a hyena at a gazelle feed — laughing and eating, laughing and eating. So, when I ripped into an enormous onion ring and felt the breading fall away into my lap, I had no one but myself to blame when my appetizer became a sizzling, onion-flavored chin strap that turned my frenzied laughing to screaming on I-5. In spite of this, I never once thought of calling a lawyer in an effort to seek damages against the fast food place and the Onion Growers of America for supplying me the means with which to be an idiot…"

Here's the response from Alabama:

> "Regarding Ned Hickson's column about jury duty, I wonder if he would think a lawsuit against him for seriously injuring or killing someone because he was eating and driving would be frivolous? The least of his problems would be a burned chin from a hot onion ring. I, for one, would LOVE to sit on that jury. He should be ashamed of his blatant disregard for others who have to share the road with him as he has his lunch."

So why am I bringing this up? I mean, aside from gathering witnesses who can be called upon in the event of my disappearance? One of the most rewarding things about being a writer is connecting with people. Elated or enraged, it means readers felt it was important enough to take time from their busy lives (not counting letters from inmates) to let you know how they feel about what you wrote.

Ultimately, isn't that what it's all about?

The same can be said for rejection letters from agents or publishing houses that include any type of hand-written comment or remark, or an emailed commentary on your work.

Even if it's NOT positive.

It's important to build a thick skin as a writer, but don't let that defensive skin become hardened to the point you stop listening. Or worse, stop appreciating.

Listening to and appreciating feedback — good or bad — can mean the difference between building a readership and losing one, building credibility among publishers or tearing it down, growing as a writer or becoming stagnant, playing dress-up when your wife is gone or finishing the next chapter.

Besides, it makes it all worthwhile when you get a comment like this one sent on a postcard from Chattanooga, Tenn.

> "Hey Mister: Yer humor has me laughfing [sic] way down in Cedar Bluff, Alabama. Drive truck for paycheck and drop off The Post newspaper all over S.E. states. Thanks for keepin' me smiling." — 'Stretch'

See? Alabama isn't all bad.

13
Avoid too much, too fast

All of us set goals.
"I'm going to lose weight."
"I'm going to drink less."
"I'm going to change careers."
"Ned is going to stop referring to himself in the third person."

Ok, maybe that last one was just me. Regardless, I think we can all agree that setting goals is important for personal improvement. However, as writers, we need to be careful about the literary goals we set — and in some cases when NOT to set them.

Some of you are probably saying, "Sure Ned, that's easy for you to say!"

Sorry, that was me speaking again, this time in second person.

Still, I think it raises a good point: I'm fortunate enough to write full-time for a newspaper, so who am I to tell you not to set lofty goals for yourself when I'm living the dream my editor coincidentally calls her nightmare?

All I can say is that I'm the guy without a college education who spent 10 years cooking in kitchens as a chef before being ~~mistakenly hired~~ enthusiastically added to the editorial staff here at *Siuslaw News* 16 years ago. I can tell you from experience that reaching this level of success, which includes as many as *five* readers from Canada, came only after making several important realizations — and experiencing failures — regarding goal setting for my writing.

Here are my top three goal-setting mistakes:

1) Waiting for Jan. 1 or some other "significant" date to get started

What I came to realize after several attempts to "start and complete that novel" was that the mere fact I was waiting for a start date doomed me to failure. I can honestly say the best things that have happened to me in my life — including meeting my wife on Match.com, getting this job, actually starting and finishing a mystery novel years ago — didn't come by way of setting goals; they came from acting on them instinctively and following through, regardless of the date. The decision to start pursuing your goals as a writer, whether it's to start a blog or publish a blockbuster, shouldn't hinge on the New Year, a birthday or when it's time to get your car's oil changed.

2) Setting goals that include things beyond your control:

There's nothing wrong with wanting to write a blockbuster and land a book deal. But don't make them *goals*. Ultimately, just like those who The Bachelor(ette) sends home (no matter how much we yell at the TV), you have no control over those kinds of things. As a writer, all you can do is focus on what you're putting on the page and have faith in what happens next. In short, set goals that relate to your realm of control — the most important of which is the quality of what you write. As with a successful restaurant, people don't come because of the place settings; they come for the food (with the possible exception of Hooters.)

Third and most important mistake to avoid…

3) Lumping too many goals together:

"I'm going to lose 30 pounds, write a novel and give up bacon!" Let's face it, if those are your goals, you're doomed once again. Why? Because while it's true that goals are supposed to be difficult and life changing, even if you could drop 30 pounds and write that novel all in the same year, what's the point if you can't eat bacon?

Whatever your goal, in order for it to be successful it needs your full attention.

One morning while diligently pumping iron from a seated position at the smoothie bar, I realized there are a number of similarities between reaching your fitness goals and writing goals — and that, in both cases, you will likely fail if you attempt too much too fast.

The same principles that make up a good fitness plan can be applied to achieving your writing goals.

Just like many people who enter the gym for the first time and are overwhelmed by the sight of dozens of different ~~torture devices designed to make you look weak and destroy your self esteem~~ pieces of fitness equipment designed to sculpt your body into lean muscle capable of opening even the most stubborn mayonnaise jar, those entering the world of writing can often be overwhelmed by their own lofty goals. They have not given themselves time to build up literary muscle before attempting to lift their lofty writing goals. It's important to ease into writing projects and commitments in a way that strengthens your writing endurance so you can avoid "injuring" your creative muscle.

This isn't to be confused with creatively injuring yourself, which I also know about. That's a whole other book.

In the same way that a smart fitness plan is built on gradual improvements through adding weight in small increments, running for longer periods or monitoring and increasing resistance in measured amounts, writers need a plan to keep their writing commitment from turning into sloppy repetitions that can hurt their goals. Any gym instructor will tell you lifting a lot of weight too quickly, or without the proper control, is pointless and even dangerous.

Especially if I'm your spotter.

The key is to recognize your limitations and commit to lifting nothing beyond that until it's time to add more.

How will you know when it's time? When you realize you're making the circuit without getting winded. In literary terms, the best measurement I can give you is this: When you find yourself easily beating your deadline(s) on a regular basis — whether self-imposed or established by an editor or agent — you're probably ready to build more muscle.

Keep working the circuit and maintaining those steady, controlled writing reps.

But please: Stay away from the gym if you're gassy.

14
Keeping your balance

Admittedly, it's very exciting to walk into a room of 50 or so booths with publishers and authors offering their latest releases and services. And when you see your own booth tucked among them, with your book cover on display and a large photo of yourself hanging on the wall behind your table, you can't help but pause and quietly think: *I have arrived as an author and, judging by its size, my nose arrived about an hour before I did*. My point is that book fairs, signings and readings are about taking the opportunity to become three-dimensional to readers, and making a connection beyond the printed page; they are about revealing yourself to people in ways that are spontaneous, real and unrehearsed, and giving them an experience they can take away and talk about with others.

My first book event led to another realization almost simultaneously: *There is no liquor at these things*.

This revelation was underscored moments later, when a 60-something woman approached my booth and began telling me how much she loved my writing, almost to the point of embarrassment. "I NEVER miss your column!" she declared. "Really – If it wasn't for your column, I doubt I would even subscribe to The Register-Guard!"

In my mind, I began pouring two fingers into a shot glass.

"Um, I write for Siuslaw News," I said with an awkward smile. "I think you're talking about Bob Welch. He's got a table right over there."

"Oh, I see…"

In that moment, if there had been an actual shot glass on the table, I'm pretty sure she would have taken it from me, chugged it, wiped her lips with one of my bookmarks and gone to see Bob. Instead, she stood immobilized and looking for a gracious exit.

"OK, actually I *am* Bob Welch," I said. "I killed Ned Hickson and have assumed his identity to expand my writing empire. If you don't tell anyone, you can help yourself to one of my books over there." I pointed to Welch's booth, which was unmanned but stacked with copies of *My Oregon*, *Pebble in the Water* and other award-winning books he's written. "If anyone asks, tell them Bob sent you," I said with a wink.

The woman, who I came to know as Joan, smiled. "So… *who* did you say you write for again?"

Those words led to my first book sale (no, it wasn't one of Bob's), and understanding the importance of meeting readers face-to-face. Even if yours wasn't the face they were looking for. During the course of six hours at my booth, I met lots of people who had no idea who I was, many of whom were drawn by my keen marketing strategy of offering a free bite of my scone for every book purchase. It was something people either reacted to with a chuckle or with a look that said, *Someone needs to let security know about you*.

As you can imagine, the corners of my scone went very fast.

At first, when I saw that some people were definitely not amused by my scone offer, I began to question the wisdom of my marketing strategy. Was it just an act of desperation in order to compete with the zombie-book guy across the way, who had creepy music, flashing lights and a mini fog machine? As I thought about this, a woman made her way to my booth, looked at my crumbling scone and shook her head.

"My husband was just here and told me about your scone," she said. "We're visiting from Arizona and our paper doesn't carry your column. Is it anything like your scone offer?"

"I'd say it's *exactly* like my scone offer," I told her. "The humor in my column is very dry."

As she bought a copy, I began to see my scone as something more than just a cranberry-flavored marketing tool. It was also a barometer of sorts, instantly gauging people's sense of humor. Those who didn't get it because of their own internal high pressure system wouldn't be happy with the book anyway. In that moment I stopped worrying about who did or didn't stop at my booth; you can't be everything to everyone.

When it came time to go to the "Authors' Reading Area," where I was supposed to read selected passages from my book, I was encouraged when I saw all the seats were filled. Some folks were even standing in the aisle! This feeling of elation was quickly followed by an even stronger feeling, which was the urge to vomit. This wasn't from fear as much as it was from advice I had been given about talking in front of a crowd:

Just picture everyone in their underwear.

This doesn't work when your mother is in the crowd. So I fixated on my wife instead, which worked well, except that I almost forgot why I was there…

I eventually got focused and read some of my favorite passages, picking up a few more sales along the way – including one from the zombie guy, who came up afterward and told me I "knocked them dead."

High praise, considering the source.

Imagine what I could do with a fog machine?

As you begin attending book-signing events, festivals, readings and other opportunities to promote your book and your writing, remember you can't be everything to everyone. You can only be yourself. Whether it's for three people who stop by your booth or a hundred people at a book signing, it's your chance to make a connection that readers will remember.

And so will you.

15

Finally, remember your superpowers

As you can probably imagine, I look really great in tights and a cape. At least on paper. In fact, all writers do! The power which writers wield with words (such as being able to use five "w" words in a row, like that) – whether (make that six) for inspiration, contemplation or revulsion – is something that elevates them to super hero status.

But, like any superhero, every writer experiences a transformation process before going into action. Sure, it doesn't involve hastily peeling off your clothes to reveal a fancy costume (depending on your genre), or a blinding flash that changes you from street clothes to colorful tights (something which could cause a problem in the newsroom.) However, while not as dramatic, there is a transformation that takes place as a writer's body language, facial expression and overall focus shifts from "earthbound" to an "alternate universe," like Asgard.

That's when, like Thor's mighty hammer, Spiderman's web-shooters, Green Lantern's ring or Hulk's endless supply of purple pants, the tools wielded by writers give them the power to get the job done. Our modern laptops, digital recorders, and notebooks lead the defense of the written word.

I realize some of you might be saying, "I don't write on a computer. I still use paper and pen. So, that's not entirely accurate."

And I suppose you'd be right. The again, Moses was technically the first person to use a tablet but let's not split hairs.

Another characteristic that writers and superheroes share is having their powers thrust upon them. Like any superhero, a writer discovers his or her gift and realizes, "With great power comes great responsibility… to pick up a second job."

Point being, there's no avoiding who you are, the powers you have been given, or the need to use them. Bruce Wayne, Peter Parker, Jean Grey, Bruce Banner, Sue Storm, Clark Kent — they all tried to deny their powers and the responsibilities they carried as a result of what fate had bestowed upon them. In each case, they came to realize they were only living within a shadow of what they were meant to be.

The same goes for writers: we ultimately embrace the action because, as I said at the very beginning of this book, we can't *not* be writers.

So, does all of this mean you should expect a call from The Justice League or Avengers?

Probably not.

But as a writer, rest assured you are in the company of a unique group of super friends.

I hope this book has helped you discover the tools you can wield as a writer, as well as the power to wield them with confidence and inspiration. While most of the eight-billion people on Earth are capable of stringing words together to communicate, it's the writers who have the power to use those words to transform a blank page into another world…

About the Author

Ned Hickson is an award-winning nationally syndicated humor columnist for *News Media Corporation*. He has been awarded "Best Local Column" from both the Oregon Newspaper Publishers Association and the Society of Professional Journalists. He is a member of the National Society of Newspaper Columnists and his weekly column appears in dozens of newspapers in the U.S. and Canada. His blog (www.NedHickson.com) is followed by more than 10,000 people who clearly have excellent taste in columnists.

Ned writes about daily life and important social issues, such as glow-in-the-dark mice and injuries caused by overheated pickles in fast food. His first book, **Humor at the Speed of Life**, was published by Port Hole Publishing in 2013 and is a collection of his most popular columns from the past decade. He is also the author of **Pearls of Writing Wisdom: From 16 Shucking Years as a Columnist**, a humorous writer's guide to survival, offering tips, insights and perspectives from his 16 years as a columnist and writer.

Ned lives in a small town on the Oregon coast with his wife, four children, two dogs, a cat and entirely too many seagulls

Because sometimes in life, you just need a good laugh. In his first book, Ned Hickson offers 16 years' worth of them.

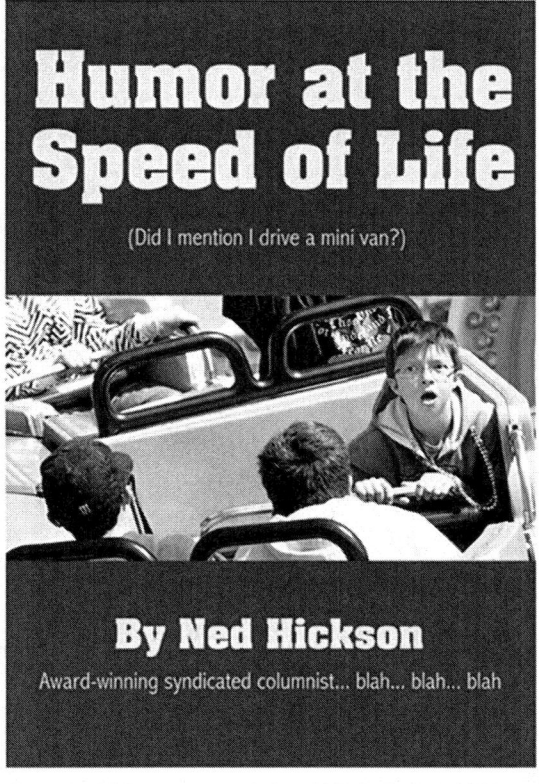

What readers and editors are saying behind Ned's back...

"It was an unexpected delight to discover a humor writer of the caliber of Dave Barry or Art Buckwald."
— Joanna Trolinger, Panama City, Fla.

"Ned Hickson gets humor and can write it. And he does so in a genre that very few do successfully."
— Scot Bolsinger Editor, Ashland Daily Tidings

"It is fascinating watching the workings of Ned Hickson's mind as he turns daily happenings into pure hilarity. Life can be very funny when viewed through his lens."
— Gay Shook Editor, Gwinette Georgia Weekly

Available at:
PortHoleBooks.com • Amazon.com • Barnes&Noble.com

The Hardly Boys: The Mystery of the Golden Goblet
by Tom Cherones

A COMEBACK FOR TEENS AT HEART! TOM CHERONES, Emmy Award winning director of the Seinfeld TV series, brings his sense of humor and narrative timing to his first novel, a delightful spoof on the old Hardy Boys classics.

Tom and Billy HARDLY, along with their chum Whit Moore, have just emerged from 50 years of sleep in a "cryogeriatrically" imposed state of suspended animation. While their bodies are now those of men in their 70s, their minds are still living in the 1950s. Their father, the famous international sleuth DeVern Hardly, is still going strong in his nineties.

Together he and "the boys" set out to locate a mysterious Golden Goblet, a priceless artifact encrusted with "jewels of all sorts: diamonds, sapphires, rubies, emeralds, and the occasional garnet." Once owned by the prominent Rosenfeld family, it had been captured by the Nazis in WWII, and then retrieved by US forces, only to be snatched from government security by dastardly criminals. Using their familiar bevy of mechanical devices (motorcycles, roadster, bi-plane, mahogany speedboat) the Hardlys set out on the trail of the *objet d'art* and the dastardly sociopath George W. Buttman and his cohorts, including the vampish Trafalgar sisters.

Their adventure takes place between studies at the local high school, where they have returned to complete their education. And what an education they receive! Confronted with technologies never dreamed of half-a-century before, they must maneuver their way through a crash course in computers, cell phones, credit cards and other "advancements." To say nothing of the "new morality," a code of behavior casually accepted by their teen contemporaries, but which they had never imagined in "their time." One hilarious episode after another brings the Hardly crew up against the challenges of their new timeframe, as they try to keep their minds on school and the overriding task at hand: solving the Mystery of the Golden Goblet.

Available from PortHoleBooks.com

Do you have a story to tell?

Port Hole Publishing
is seeking entertaining, educational,
wholesome material to publish.
Let us know if you have the next
great novel languishing in a drawer,
a personal memoir or researched
topic to put in print.

Contact us through our website:
PortHolePublications.com

*We bring over 40 years of
experience to our projects.*